HOUSEPLANTS
& BOTTLE GARDENS

■ Step by Step to Growing Success ■

Ian Murray

CROWOOD GARDENING GUIDES

First published in 1991 by
The Crowood Press Ltd
Ramsbury, Marlborough
Wiltshire SN8 2HR

British Library Cataloguing in Publication Data

Murray, Ian
    Houseplants and bottle gardens.
    1. Indoor plants
    1. Title
    635.965

ISBN 1 85223 504 7

Picture credits
Line-drawings by Claire Upsdale-Jones

Typeset by Avonset, Midsomer Norton, Bath
Printed and bound by Times Publishing Group, Singapore

Contents

Acknowledgements

I think I would like to have been a plant hunter, voyaging around the world in search of unknown species, but I was born too late. Not that everything has been discovered, far from it, but natural habitats are being destroyed so quickly that flora and fauna are becoming extinct before they can be discovered. Tragically, much has been lost before it has been seen, let alone evaluated and appreciated. As an alternative to travelling in far-off lands though, I heartily recommend a journey amongst the people who make a living from plants, and who grow them for fun.

During my recent travels, whilst preparing this book, I met many plantspeople and I would like to record my appreciation for the help which I received. They are Allan Long of Mansell and Hatcher's orchid nursery, and Jim Speed and John Ravenscroft of Bridgemere Garden World.

Thanks also to Mary Cawood at the Van Zelst nurseries in Knaresborough, and to Terry Davison for demonstrating the craft of making terrariums. I am also grateful to Wyevale Garden Centres for photographic facilities, to the Saint-paulia and Houseplant Society for its help and to Richard Haynes of the British Orchid Council for his assistance. Special thanks are due to Diana Morphett for the opportunity to see her plant collection and to Barbara Potter for the warmth of her hospitality, and the excellence of her fruit crumble!

Finally and humbly, I must pay tribute to my wife Kathy and her great tolerance. She gives substance to the old adage that . . . 'Behind every man who writes, there is a woman who wrongs'.

Introduction

Human beings and every other form of life owe their continued existence to plants of every description, but it is only quite recently that this realization has begun to have a strong impact. Vegetation is and always has been the only source of food because no other organism is capable of transforming solar energy so that it can be used by living creatures. Not only that, but current concern about the 'greenhouse effect' has focused our attention on the role plants play in maintaining a favourable atmospheric balance.

This situation is not universally recognized but nonetheless, human make-up does seem to contain an element which acknowledges the importance of our flora. Even in urban society, away from the realities of the natural world, there is a strong affinity with plants. Their form and beauty are admired and throughout the history of mankind, their decorative and symbolic uses have always been evident; nowadays, civilization has reached a sophisticated level of growing crops and attention has been diverted from necessities to aesthetics. Farming used to involve most of the population but since it became almost completely mechanized, man's contact with plants has been confined to gardening and this has become an enormously popular leisure activity. The emphasis is on the creation of beautiful surroundings and even where gardens are present, plants have joined man in his home.

When plants were first brought indoors from their natural habitats (during the sixteenth century at the behest of European aristocracy) they were initially housed in specially constructed buildings which gradually developed into the greenhouse. This protection was necessary because the plants were invariably tropical, sought by intrepid collectors in distant and inaccessible parts of the world. The acquisition of hitherto unknown plants became fashionable amongst the rich, and their patronage was instrumental in expanding botanical knowledge and establishing major collections. Gradually, the lure of cultivation spread through society and during the Industrial Revolution, for instance, mill and factory workers became renowned for raising decorative plants. Thereafter the fascination spread until it reached today's huge proportions.

The relationship between man and indoor plants is difficult to explain but may hark back to the time when we lived in the wild, in forests and woods. In addition, plants undoubtedly have a therapeutic effect, and of course their flowers can be beautiful, their branches architecturally delightful, their foliage handsome and colourful. Whatever your need, plants can considerably add interest to, and even transform a home. The need for decoration is an obvious human characteristic and the major outlet is definitely the home where plants can readily fulfil this ornamental function either as individual features or on the grander scale of a living interior display. Whether as an aid to the psyche or the décor, or simply something to be nurtured, the important thing is that plants give tremendous pleasure and my hope is that this book will further that end.

There are many different ways of raising indoor plants from controlling a mini, sophisticated environment to tending the standard terracotta pot. But whatever your choice I am sure that enjoyment is increased by success, and to this end some knowledge is required. So, to begin at the beginning, let us look at what a plant is and understand its lifestyle.

CHAPTER 1

Being a Plant

Like every other form of life, plants have evolved over millions of years adapting to and taking advantage of their environment. Stable local conditions are essential to their well-being and if climatic, or other conditions, change rapidly (in other words, within a few thousand years) they are unable to respond. Plants, unlike animals, cannot forage for food or water during a drought. They die. Living beings can only change their characteristics by the process of natural selection and these changes do not take place in individuals but only in the species as a whole. Certainly plants are adaptable within a range of conditions – some more than others – but if the environment quickly becomes unfavourable they are unable to make a positive response.

This is the crux of all problems which prevent houseplants from succeeding. In fact, the very name 'houseplant' is misleading because it implies that these particular plants are suited for life in the home. We often find it difficult to appreciate that although a house is a human sanctuary, it can be exceedingly hostile to plant life. History does not record whether primeval man tried to cultivate plants in the cave or hut, but we know that failure would have resulted. More recent generations did introduce some species into their home, but only with partial success. Noxious fumes from gas lights and coal fires, very low light levels, and the often huge winter temperature difference between day and night meant plants had a difficult time. Such problems were compounded because our forefathers were ignorant of many of the scientific principles which we now take for granted. Nevertheless, their persistence brought some success and many people will have memories of the aspidistra in

the parlour, stoically resisting the prevailing conditions and surviving the frequent doses of cigarette ash and tea leaves.

The aspidistra gives an important clue about the nature of plants. Some are more tolerant than others, but if you want them to flourish you must determine their likes and dislikes. Each individual species was fashioned by its immediate surroundings so knowledge of the natural habitat is invaluable. However, there are fundamental influences which are common to all plants and these need consideration before specific preferences are noted.

THE ENVIRONMENT
Temperature

Plants have managed to inhabit most areas of the planet, from the deserts to the polar fringes, but vegetation cannot exist where there is permanent ice. Life processes depend on the movement of liquids from cell to cell, and obviously this is impossible where temperatures are markedly below the freezing point of water. Plants, like some animals, cannot raise their own temperature above ambient levels although they are able to reduce it when water evaporates from the leaves. On the other hand, some highly specialized plants succeed in unbelievably hot areas and one example is *Weltwitschia*, which is found in the Namib Desert of south-west Africa. This incredible plant can withstand surface temperatures of 70°C(l58°F), too hot even to touch. I would add that it is not an attractive specimen and looks rather like a piece of wrinkled leather, but still it is a remarkable survivor.

In the home a temperature range of 15–27°C (60–80°F) would be satisfactory for most house-plants, especially if this were fairly constant. The advent of central heating makes this entirely possible, but it is general practice to allow the system to go off at night when the temperature may fall to 10°C (50°F) or even lower. For many tropical plants, this is a critical temperature – anything below is fatal, even for just a short period.

Light

The sun's radiation, direct or indirect, is used in a process called photosynthesis to manufacture food within the plant. Depending where the plants originate it also determines their re-quirements. Everywhere on earth receives the same amount of daylight over a 12-month period, whether it be the 6 months of day and 6 months of night in the poles, or the 12 hours of day and night at the equator. However, there is a tremendous difference in the intensity of light between these two extremes, and there is the additional variation in the amount of cloud cover. Different plant species have evolved to accom-modate varying light intensities. Whereas cacti and other near-desert flora can tolerate almost ceaseless direct sunshine, those from dense forest need subdued light and would be damag-ed by strong sunlight.

The period of illumination is critical to some plants because it initiates certain responses, par-ticularly where flowering is concerned. The chrysanthemum and poinsettia are examples of 'short day' subjects which will only flower naturally when day length shortens, and fuchsias are 'long day' plants, only coming into bloom when the days exceed a certain length. In the home natural light is scarce and uncontrollable, while artificial illumination does not significantly help plants to grow. The natural light, of course, only comes through windows which means that in most cases it is from one direction. It is obvious that the brightest places in the home are the windowsills, but is less well known that 1.5m (5ft)

Fig 1   Eustoma in purple and white.

away, the light intensity may be three or four times less.

Unfortunately human beings are poor judges of light levels because the eyes have a compen-sating device, the iris, which opens wider in poor light and closes in strong light. Photographers will know how poorly lit a lounge is compared to the outdoors, but plants have an even greater awareness because their life support systems depend on it. Home growers must learn to recognize the different light zones and use them to accommodate the varying requirements of houseplants or, alternatively, provide good artificial illumination.

Water

The question most asked about plants for the home is, 'How often should they be watered?' The answer, while wholly accurate, is unhelpful . . . 'When they need it.' It would be much simpler if a firm timetable could be given for this troublesome procedure but, alas, there are too many variables. What kind of plant and how large is it? What time of year is it? Is the plant in active growth? What is the ambient temperature and humidity? In fact the secret of successful watering is no secret at all – it depends on experience (or sympathetic intuition). There are those who wield a watering can with sublime accuracy, as though they were responding to telepathic messages, but in the hands of most people that same can is a weapon of destruction. Without any doubt the most common cause of premature death amongst houseplants is excessive watering, a cruel irony born out of kindness. Studied neglect is often the better course of action.

Most plants can store water for short periods and some can do so for years, but when the limit of endurance is reached they wilt. This is a proper response because it actually reduces further water loss and unless the deprivation is prolonged, the plant recovers perfectly when it is watered. Sadly, over-watering cannot be rectified. Roots also need air to remain healthy and if they are kept permanently wet, the precious gases are precluded – and dead roots mean dead plants. Ideally compost should be permanently moist without being wet, but this state is almost impossible to maintain in a plant pot. The only alternative is to water thoroughly and then allow the compost to become practically dry before watering again. Again, it all depends on the plant; some are semi-aquatic and are almost impossible to kill with excess water, whilst others should not be watered at all for long periods. However, the great majority of houseplants are best served by a regime which ensures that the roots are dry for short periods, or almost so.

Air

The importance of air to plant roots has been mentioned, but oxygen and carbon dioxide are also a vital part of photosynthesis and are as available indoors as outdoors. However, another gas which may not be appreciated as such is water vapour, and its presence is essential to most plants. When water evaporates it becomes a gas and thus part of the air; we call this humidity and, in varying degrees, it is necessary for healthy vegetation. With special exceptions like cacti and succulents – which have evolved into efficient water-saving structures and are immune to the effects of dry air – most plants need to be enveloped in moist air. Centrally-heated rooms are usually too dry, even for humans, and the arid atmosphere certainly makes life difficult for indoor plants.

Leaves, as well as releasing oxygen and carbon dioxide, give off water vapour which helps to reduce the temperature of the plant and causes replacement water to be taken up by the roots. If the surrounding air is humid (in other words, moist), the rate of water loss is reduced, but if it is very dry plants may lose moisture faster than it can be replaced, even if the roots are kept in wet soil. This question is hard to comprehend but, broadly speaking, the higher the temperature the more moist the air should be. And the warmer the atmosphere, the more moisture it can hold, although in the home there is rarely any such moisture.

It is hardly likely that even the most ardent cultivator would fill a lounge with humidifiers and bowls of water. Plants might enjoy these conditions but the same is not true of wallpaper, carpets and upholstery. Clearly some compromise is needed and there are only two realistic alternatives. First, sensitive plants can be grown in glass enclosures which will favour them exclusively or they can be placed where a more humid microclimate can be created. The usual message is to spray foliage with water, but desirable though this may be, the effect is short-lived. A more helpful technique involves using a tray or

Fig 2   Left to right, 'on the television': Neanthe bella *(parlour palm);* Peperomia magnoliaefolia *(desert privet);* Asparagus plumosus *(asparagus fern).*

shallow dish containing pebbles and water, on which the plants are placed to benefit from the localized and constant evaporation. It is important that the pots are either on small saucers or that the water level is below the top of the pebbles, otherwise the compost will quickly become saturated. The water will obviously need to be replenished from time to time.

There is one other method of improving humidity and that involves growing plants in groups so that each benefits from the transpired water vapour of its neighbours.

Plant Locations

The majority of houseplants are grown in the living-room which is unquestionably the most hostile location in the house. In summer, when the heating is off, conditions are fairly satisfactory but in winter, if the room is comfortably heated, many plants will be distressed. Short days mean a meagre amount of light, and domestic lighting does little to stimulate the plants which are receiving two contradictory messages. The low light levels say remain dormant, and the temperature says grow. Understandably the plant's metabolism is upset and the result is usually inferior growth. However, with precautions there are species which can tolerate this situation, but there is no wisdom in wasting money and attention on those which will inevitably succumb. The windowsill, behind drawn curtains, is another microclimate which will suit some plants, but remember that on a frosty night, even with double glazing, the temperature will drop sufficiently to be fatal to most tropical plants.

The kitchen is the next most popular and is a more agreeable plant site. Normally it is not as

Fig 3   Flan dishes or large plates will serve as humidity trays — just add pea gravel and water. The combined thermometer/hygrometer is an optional extra which can be exceptionally helpful.

hot as the lounge, and cooking and washing activities ensure that the air is much more humid. Consequently, although free surfaces are at a premium, plants have a good chance of remaining healthy. The hall and landing are next on the list and for many households these are priority locations, but not without their difficulties. When these areas are heated in the winter, it is usually at a reasonably low level so that the main obstacle to successful growing will be the poor illumination.

Many homes have a combined living and dining room and often the latter area is kept at a lower temperature than the rest of the room which means that reasonable warmth prevails. If there is a separate dining room this may only be heated for meal times, and for the rest of the day and night it will be one of the coolest areas during the winter. The bathroom is undoubtedly the best place of all for plants because of the relatively high humidity and the fact that it is usually kept gently warm. Glossy magazines often give

Fig 4   There is no need to use the best dishes for gravel trays because they are mostly concealed when the plants (Begonia rex and Syngonium in this case) are in place.

illustrated ideas for plant décor, and I do believe that home gardeners should give more con-

sideration to using the bathroom as a prime site. It gives the only opportunity in the house to grow those delicate subjects which require coddling, and is also an excellent recovery zone for houseplants which may have been suffering elsewhere. Bedrooms are where fewest plants are found and this is almost certainly due to the belief that it is unhealthy to grow them there. It is true that plants use oxygen at night but even a bedroom packed with vegetation would not cause any problems. On the other hand, allergy sufferers should not contemplate putting flowering plants in the bedroom.

It goes without saying that conservatories are the ideal location for plants of every description. They are a marvellous hybrid between the greenhouse and the lounge, and any plant lover who is thinking of a home extension should consider them. Conservatories give a real opportunity to live with plants on their terms, but without compromising the comforts which humans hold so dear. They do, however, fall outside the scope of this book.

In concluding this chapter, I acknowledge that it contains a certain amount of technical information which may come as a surprise to new gardeners. However, I am sure that if certain principles are appreciated, the cultivation of indoor plants will be more successful and enjoyable. Gardening is a creative pursuit underpinned by immutable scientific facts.

CHAPTER 2

Open-Room Cultivation

Despite the fact that houseplants can be grown far more successfully in various glass enclosures, in the vast majority of homes they occupy windowsills, shelves and table tops. The drawbacks have already been outlined, but it cannot be emphasized too much that for most vegetation the home is one of the most difficult places for successful growth, or even survival. Certainly there are a few species which can give a good account of themselves but, broadly speaking, houses are unfit places for houseplants. In most cases the premature demise of a fine specimen is attributable to over-watering, but this disguises the fact that low humidity and inferior lighting eventually take their toll. Over-watering causes a fairly rapid death, whereas the other factors lead more slowly to the same inevitable end.

The wisest course of action is to decide where the plant is to be placed and then choose from a range of plants which have the best chance of survival in that position. It seems futile to buy on impulse and then hope that the admired

Fig 5   A group planting in a wooden container allowing each plant to benefit from the proximity of another. Those shown include a devil's ivy, dumb cane, rabbit tracks, polka dot and a creeping fig.

Fig 6   A bowl planting dominated by grape ivy, and a maidenhair fern
with support from Begonia rex and a variegated ivy.

Fig 7 Howea *palm, variegated rubber plant,* Scindapsus, *and* Dieffenbachia, *make up this display in a self-watering container. There is a water level indicator and a reservoir which periodically requires topping up.*

Fig 8 *Each of these plants succeeds in a lounge but please note that this is a summer picture and the radiator is not in use.* Fatshedera *is in front with* Rademachera *and* Schefflera *behind.*

purchase will somehow remain a flourishing specimen – this can only be a waste of money leading to considerable disappointment. While it is believed that plants can adapt to different conditions, the truth is that the majority can only do so within very narrow limits.

The three variables of temperature, light and humidity are the determining influences, and all are controllable to some extent, although not always conveniently. Few home growers will adjust the warmth of a room to suit the resident flora. In winter, the increased cold can easily kill a plant. There are various light zones in the home where suitable plants can be grown, but remember that a shady area in summer will be positively dark during the winter. Surprisingly, few people make much use of the benefits available from supplementary lighting, although the results are highly decorative as well as conducive to healthy plant growth.

Humidity is a more difficult matter and although there has been a steady increase in the sales of room humidifiers, they are usually purchased to benefit humans and not plants. The use of plant gravel trays is, I believe, essential for anyone who wishes to extend the range of plants which can be maintained in good condition. Individual plants can also be placed in very attractive plantholders, and if the space between the pot and the plantholder is filled with moist peat, the microclimate is improved. Plants grouped together will enjoy a more moist atmosphere, created by the emission of water vapour from the surrounding leaves.

Another effective strategy is to give houseplants a regular period of convalescence during

Fig 9   If a pot plant is placed in a larger plantholder and surrounded by moist peat, it will increase local humidity.

talented growers who achieve remarkable results. They instinctively monitor the health of their collection and seem able to identify the best locations in the house and the correct treatment. Unfortunately, instruction in the acquisition of instincts is fruitless and my conclusions are that 'natural' cultivators are the product of accumulated experience and possess innate observational skills.

Talking to plants may be important, but we just do not know. Apparently, someone in America attached the electrodes of a lie-detector to parts of a plant and subjected it to various stimuli – aggressive and conciliatory language as well as different kinds of music. Positive responses were reported but the results have not been scientifically verified. On top of that you have to ask

Fig 10   Two of the great survivors of 'open room' cultivation – Ficus robusta and Tolmeia menziesii.

which they can recover from the tribulations of being confined in a building which is designed, built and maintained for a completely different life form. Where a greenhouse or conservatory can be used, the rest cure can be effected at most times of the year as long as the minimum temperature is within the range suitable to the plant. During the temperate parts of the spring and for the whole summer, even the most exotic species will relish equable outdoor humidity, fresh air, abundant light and soothing rain. A sheltered spot in partial shade is most beneficial, while strong sunshine and wind must be avoided; so too must the chilly nights which are not uncommon even in the midst of a heatwave.

Despite everything which I have said about the difficulties of growing plants in the home, it must be acknowledged that there is a legion of would *Cissus antarctica* prefer Vaughan Williams to aboriginal music, and can we assume that the *Aspidistra* likes heavy metal bands? I would also shrink from confronting my plants with a pruning knife, vainly pleading that the surgery was beneficial. The future may bring some surprises but until then I think we should rely on tried and tested techniques, and I am sure that armed with the knowledge of a particular plant's natural habitat we should endeavour to simulate the correct conditions. This approach, I believe, gives the best chance of success and fulfilment.

So far I may have been guilty of emphasizing the obstacles and perplexities of domestic cultivation, and so as we begin to examine specific plants for specific purposes the accent should be on encouragement and positive achievement. The listings of plants in the following chapters include information about preferred conditions, but first the categories need a brief explanation.

NOTES ON PLANT LISTINGS

Minimum Temperature

This is the figure below which the plant will suffer, but an occasional drop beyond the minimum will not normally be harmful especially if the compost is fairly dry. Most of the species which concern us are temperate, sub-tropical or tropical, but even the few which are hardy should not be subjected to frost.

Light Zones

The guidance on light levels is necessarily arbitrary and imprecise but recognizes the difficulty of identifying the degree of brightness or shade. Therefore, only four categories are used to indicate plant preferences. The vast majority of those plants listed will not tolerate direct sunshine in the summer but might benefit from a sunny spot in winter.

1. Some sun. This describes positions where

plants might receive direct sunlight for a few hours each day.
2. Bright. A situation where there is never any direct sunshine but is otherwise the brightest spot in the room. Rooms that receive more light than others should house plants, particularly in winter, when bright conditions only are required. More tolerant subjects will be identified as 'bright/partial shade'.
3. Partial shade. Most of the room will probably fall into this category which describes places receiving some direct light from windows, without sunshine. Usually they are half-way from the window to the centre of the room.
4. Shade. Only a few plants thrive in such conditions which might be in the corners of bright rooms, or in the centre of rooms with a northerly aspect.

The use of comparative terms is obviously imprecise but houses and rooms differ enormously in the amount of light which is available and only the home gardener can make a proper assessment. Experience will be the best guide, and for newcomers to growing I suggest a trial run in various sites with some of the inexpensive members of the top ten survivors group.

TOP TEN SURVIVORS

The plants listed here are exceedingly tough and easy to care for and, as such, can be considered ideal subjects for inexperienced growers or those who have a sad history of killing houseplants.

Aspidistra (cast-iron plant) – thrives in poor light and a wide range of temperatures.
Cissus antarctica (kangaroo vine) – good in shade and in warm or cold rooms.
Crassula argentea (jade plant) – a sunny or bright position suits it best.
Fatshedera (ivy tree) – combines the ruggedness of *Fatsia* and ivy.
Fatsia japonica (castor oil plant) – cool is best but indifferent to light or shady positions.

Neanthe bella (parlour palm) – enjoys room conditions and fairly dry compost.

Rhoicissus rhomboidea (grape ivy) – looks and behaves like the *Cissus*.

Sansevieria trifasciata (mother-in-law's tongue) – prefers sun or brightness but tolerates some shade.

Tolmiea menziesii (piggy-back plant) – all the better for coolness, and adaptable to various light levels.

Yucca elephantipes (spineless yucca) – likes maximum light and cool winters.

I hesitate to describe these ten plants as indestructible but they are certainly able to withstand considerable neglect and abuse. As I have said elsewhere, neglect in moderation is actually a positive help in enabling houseplants to survive, but abuse is more dangerous. All the listed plants are happier in cool rooms, especially in the winter when they are semi-dormant, and cool can be said to include 'cold' as long as the temperature is well above freezing. The winter is also the time when watering is critical, and tolerant though these plants may be they will suffer if watering is excessive. Remember that during this season they are resting and therefore only sufficient water is required to maintain their reduced metabolic needs. Even though the top of the compost may be dry, observation of the plants will show that they are entirely happy, drawing their minimal needs from within the rooting medium where it is still slightly moist. In a room with low levels of heating, or none at all, this equilibrium will exist for some weeks, and despite the anxiety which may afflict the caring cultivator, the urge to water must be resisted.

In summer the situation is completely different and whilst the plants are actively growing they will use more water and, perhaps more importantly, are better able to cope with excess. However, even when more watering is needed, it is still most important to allow the compost to become dry, or almost so, before watering again.

If this regime is adhered to I am tempted to offer written guarantees for the survival of the 'top ten' and in addition, I will vouchsafe that each will become a specimen to admire. They may be good survivors but they are also capable of becoming, and remaining, very handsome subjects.

OPEN-ROOM FOLIAGE PLANTS

Before considering those subjects which will benefit most from the protection of cabinets and other glass enclosures, we will examine the plants which are most often at the mercy of ordinary room conditions and can give a good account of themselves.

Acorus gramineus 'Variegatus' (sweet flag, myrtle grass). Min 4.5°C(40°F). Bright/partial shade. This is not a plant of great beauty but the white-striped, grassy leaves add a note of variety to plant collections. The compost should always be kept moist and even wet in summer.

Araucaria excelsa (Norfolk Island pine). Min 7.5°C(45°F). Bright/partial shade. An evergreen conifer which is particularly attractive whilst young, but it does tend to lose lower leaves and branches as it matures. It is better kept in a small container and only repotted every couple of years. Whilst this will help to restrict its growth, it also means frequent use of the watering can in summer.

Aspidistra elatior (cast-iron plant). Min 4.5°C (40°F). Bright/partial shade/shade. Dragged from its native China and imprisoned in Victorian parlours, the *Aspidistra* never complained and thoroughly justified its popular name. After being the butt of many jokes and surviving spent tea leaves and cigarette ash, it is becoming fashionable again though ironically not easy to obtain. If watered moderately in summer and less frequently in winter it can become a handsome specimen. There is a somewhat rare variegated version.

Fig II   A very tough subject which will add
some cheer to a shady spot is Aucuba
japonica 'Variegata' (spotted laurel). It is quite
hardy and will prefer lower temperatures.

Fig I2   Two plants with 'grass-like' foliage
which add a touch of upright elegance to plant
displays. Carex morrowi (left) and Acorus
gramineus (right), with Asparagus plumosus in
between.

Aucuba japonica 'Variegata' (spotted laurel). Min
4.5°C(40°F). Partial shade/shade. A most useful
and cheerful looking foliage plant for gloomy parts
of the house, especially where it is also cool. Leaves
will soon drop in hot and dry conditions, but
otherwise Aucuba will thrive; probably needs
occasional pruning to keep in check.

Carex morrowii 'Variegata' (Japanese sedge).
Min 7.5°C(45°F). Sun/bright/partial shade.
Whereas Acorus is straight leaved, the Japanese
sedge has a lovely arching habit and is extremely
tolerant of good or poor light conditions. The
compost should be permanently moist, though it
does not seem to mind occasional dryness or
even saturated roots.

Chamaerops humilis (European fan palm). Min
7.5°C(45°F). Bright/partial shade. The only palm

which is indigenous to Europe will grace any
room which is not excessively warm in the
winter. If it is repotted only rarely it will take
years before it becomes large. A well-drained
compost is important; liberal watering in the
winter will put this plant under stress.

Chlorophytum comosum 'Variegatum' (spider
plant). Min 7.5°C(45°F). Bright/partial shade.
Away from intense sunlight the spider plant will
give a superb show and is especially suitable for
an interior hanging basket. Although it hails from
South Africa it is remarkably adaptable to varying light levels (note the variegation is more prominent in brightness though). The small plantlets
which appear at the end of wiry stems can be left
on the mother plant or used for propagation.

Cissus antarctica (kangaroo vine). Min 7.5°C

Fig 13   The adaptability of Chlorophytum (spider plant) is well known; many examples are also very beautiful.

Fig 14   A sunny or at least very bright position will suit the jade plant to perfection, but remember that it is Crassula argentea, a succulent, and must be virtually dry at the roots during its winter rest.

(50°F). Partial shade. Some confusion of nomenclature has existed with this genus and *Rhoicissus*, but the kangaroo vine comfortably inhabits many homes and is surprisingly perky, even in very shady spots. Two relatives are worthy of mention. *C. discolor* is a climbing/trailing plant with such strikingly coloured leaves as to deserve the popular name of rex begonia vine, and *C. striata* is a beautiful trailer whose young leaves are pink, turning dark green as they age. Both are less resilient than *C. antarctica*.

Crassula argentea (jade plant). Min 7.5°C (45°F). Sun/bright. Most cacti and succulents, though fascinating and various, tend to be considered more as curiosities than as aesthetically

pleasing plants. Consequently, only a few are listed in this book. However, the jade plant is one which cannot be ignored because it is permanently handsome and has superb survival characteristics. It quickly takes on a tree-like shape and the fleshy, lustrous green leaves have what appears to be a red glow around the edges. Only excess water, coupled with low temperatures, will put this *Crassula* out of its stride. Virtual dryness during the winter months is highly desirable.

Dracaena. Min 13°C(55°F).   Bright/partial shade. Variously described as the dragon tree or

Fig 15   There are probably more different varities of Dracaena than any
other foliage plant, and many have outstanding combinations of leaf
colours and markings. The photograph shows D. 'Golden King'.

Fig 16 Dracaena 'Albertii'.

false palm. Some of this genus are spectacular foliage plants but only two species, *D. marginata* (Madagascar dragon tree) and its tricolour version are entirely happy in dry air, although *D. draco* is similarly resistant. Perversely the most colourful *Dracaena*, such as *D. terminalis* and its various versions, require higher humidity and are unlikely to remain attractive for long in the normal living room.

D. *indivisa*, more properly called *Cordyline australis*, is often used to provide an exotic touch in summer bedding displays and will survive quite low temperatures, but this species does demand bright light. *Pleomele reflexa* (song of India) is a delightful plant and is now officially included in the genus *Dracaena*. It has lovely golden leaves with a hint of green, but is much less likely to be found than its variegated counterpart; both are very slow growing. One other species to mention is *D. sanderiana* which has much smaller leaves than the others, and an upright growth

habit. It is a good subject for cabinets and bottles.

Eucalyptus globulus (gum tree). Min 7.5°F (40°F). Bright/sun. The cedar gum and lemon-scented gum are widely cultivated but *E. globulus* is the most popular. The latter reaches 45m (150ft) in its Australian homeland and as a house-plant it will soon outgrow its welcome. Pinching out the growing tips will delay its vertical aspirations and will also promote more juvenile leaves which are the most attractive feature.

Euonymus (Japanese spindle tree). Min 4.5°C (40°F). Bright/partial shade. There are several

Fig 17 Dracaena 'Santa Rosa'.

21

variegated types from which to choose and all are quite slow growing, especially in small pots. The leaves are quite tough, but they will undoubtedly drop if the plant is kept warm in the winter.

Fatshedera lizie (ivy tree). Min 4.5°C(40°F). Bright/partial shade. A hybrid produced from *Hedera* and *Fatsia*. It is a permanently good-looking plant with glossy, five-lobed leaves. Like *Euonymus* it is usually sold as three or four cuttings per pot. *Fatshedera* grows as a natural but slow climber – if the growing tips are removed, quite bushy specimens will result. Tolerance is a prime characteristic of these plants but it is advisable to keep them out of centrally-heated rooms in the winter.

Fatsia japonica (castor oil plant). Min 4.5°C (40°F). Bright/partial shade. It has been popular in homes for even longer than the *Aspidistra* with which it shares a justified reputation for survival and durability. A well-grown specimen can reach 90–120cm (3–4 ft), but is easily restrained by pinching the tips or occasional pruning. Excessive winter warmth should be avoided as should liberal winter watering.

Ficus (fig tree, rubber plant). Min 10°C(50°F). Bright/partial shade. The ornamental fig family includes quite a few highly successful houseplants whose robust leaves are adept at resisting the atmospheric dryness of the home. What was formerly the ordinary rubber plant is now available in several varieties, some with variegated foliage, and for many growers the main question is what to do when it reaches the ceiling. *F. benjamina* (weeping fig), is a most elegant small tree and the variegated versions are magnificent; the trailing species of *Ficus* need

Fig 19 Ficus benjamina *(weeping fig), can grow to 1.8m (6ft). This one has had its stems 'plaited' and is in a self-watering container.*

Fig 18 Ficus benjamina *'Starlight' in a wall-mounted plantholder where its arching growth is seen to advantage.*

22

Fig 20 A marvellous specimen of the variegated weeping fig.

more humidity and are better grown in bottle gardens and terraria.

Grevillea robusta (silk oak). Min 7.5°F(45°F). Bright. Another Australian tree which grows quite quickly and whose evergreen leaves lose their elegance when the plant is older. When it reaches about 90cm(3ft) the silk oak is better discarded and replaced by a seedling (which is easily raised).

Hedera (common ivy, English ivy). Min 4.5°C (40°F). Bright/partial shade. There are numerous named varieties of *H. helix*, with interesting leaf markings, which bely the name common ivy. All will succeed away from a centrally-heated room with its associated dryness. They climb readily if support is provided, or trail from hanging con-

tainers, and whilst they are not star performers they are excellent in a group which includes more glamorous plants.

Helxine (mind your own business). Min 7.5°C (45°F). Bright/partial shade. A highly adaptable, creeping plant which some people might class as an indoor weed. If the compost is always moist, *Helxine* will certainly spread wildly. Consequently, it is not ideally placed beside other small but less vigorous subjects.

Heptapleurum arboricola (parasol plant). Min 13°C(55°F). Bright. Relatively unknown until recently and often confused with *Schefflera*. Its main advantage over the latter is that removing the growing point will induce quite bushy growth. There is a most appealing variegated form but, as with many such plants, the leaf markings disappear from later growth if the light levels are too low.

Howea forsteriana (Kentia palm). Min 10°C (50°F). Partial shade. Named after Lord Howe Island in the South Pacific, the Kentia palm has a rugged constitution and, like the parlour palm, acquits itself well in murky situations. It, too, benefits from dormancy in the winter when the temperature should not exceed 16°C(60°F) and the compost must be kept fairly dry.

Monstera delicosa (Swiss cheese plant). Min 10°C(50°F). Partial shade. If you want a plant to grow from the hallway to landing, clinging as it goes, then *Monstera* is the right choice although I know that it is not universally admired. The huge leaves can look out of place and the aerial roots are obtrusive, but it does seem to earn the affection of those who grow it.

Neanthe bella (parlour palm). Min 10°C(50°F). Partial shade. Cool winters and a moderately dry compost will ensure the survival of this inexpensive palm. Its main attributes are modest stature, slow growth, and tolerance of low light levels. It is often labelled *Chamaedorea elegans*.

Fig 21   A Helxine *in small pot, but note it is a vigorous grower.*

Fig 22   *A very clean specimen of* Monstera.

Philodendron   Min 13°C(55°F). Partial shade. A large family of plants which will live in warm homes and, because they have tough leaves, there is some immunity from dry air. They do, however, prefer reasonable humidity to look their best. *P. scandens* (sweetheart plant) is the most popular of the climbing types, and *P. bipinnatifidum* (tree philodendron) is the most common of the upright growers. There are two with interesting leaf colour – 'Burgundy' and *P. melanochryson* ('Black Gold'). Winter warmth is essential for the *Philodendron* and, if the atmosphere is not arid, they survive very well.

Plectranthus (Swedish ivy). Min 10°C(50°F). Bright/partial shade. Three species make good houseplants because they tolerate dry air although each has a different light requirement. *P. coleoides marginatus* (candle plant) is a bright subject for bright conditions, and anything but the fiercest sunshine is suitable. *P. australis* is for semi-shade and does well in quite murky positions. *P. oertendahlii* has white veined leaves and

Fig 23 *The bright foliage of* Plectranthus coleoides *'Variegata' looks at its best on a windowsill which receives at least a few hours of sun each day.*

likes good light without direct sunshine. The candle plant is upright with a tendency towards arching growth whilst the other two are trailers.

Podocarpus macrophyllus (bhuddist pine). Min 4.5°C(40°F). Bright/some sunshine. An upright grower with narrow, glossy leaves and a cheerful acceptance of cold conditions; it is also slow growing though occasional pruning may be necessary for reshaping. The bhuddist pine is quite uncommon and comes from China and Japan.

Radermachera Min 10°C(50°F). Bright/partial shade. A relative newcomer as an indoor plant which is more properly named *Stereosperum chelonoides*. An evergreen and fairly quick-growing tree it has small, glossy, dark green

leaves and in the short time it has been available gives every indication of having a rugged constitution. Whilst young it is well proportioned, but when it reaches 60cm(2ft) high, the leaf stems elongate giving a rather sparse appearance. Although I recommended 10°C(50°F) as a minimum temperature, the plants which I grow seem undaunted by 4.5°C(40°F) and the foliage lasts well in a variety of light conditions.

Rhoicissus Min 7.5°C(45°F). Bright/partial shade. Like the *Cissus* group of plants these are climbing vines and include *R. rhomboidea* which has the misleading common name of grape ivy. However, it has a justified reputation as a robust but unremarkable foliage subject which will prosper in sun or shade, and all situations in between these extremes. Close relations, *R. capensis*, (Cape grape) and *R. rhombifolius* (mermaid vine) have similar requirements except that they prefer slightly warmer quarters for the winter.

Fig 24 *Rhoicissus rhomboidea (grape ivy), is a natural climber, but it makes a happy trailing plant in a wall-mounted plantholder. It is surprisingly effective in quite murky corners.*

25

Sansevieria (mother-in-law's tongue). Min 10°C(50°F). Bright/partial shade. The best-looking example of this genus is *S. trifasciata* 'Laurentii' which has dark, horizontal markings on the leaves which are edged with yellow. Everything about this plant suggests toughness and indeed the fibres were once used to make bow strings by tropical African tribesmen. Un-affected by dry air, *Sansevieria* does have an Achilles' heel – sustained low temperatures and over-watering in the winter will lead to rotting roots and leaves. Grown well they will last for years and clusters of small, scented flowers will appear annually. The leaves of mature specimens may reach more than 60cm(2ft) in height, but there is a dwarf species *S. hahnii* which forms a rosette of 10cm (4in) long leaves, useful for bottles and plant cases.

Fig 25 A mature Schefflera *is an impressive sight, reaching 1.7m (5.5ft) in height. The variegated variety shown is the 'Gold Cap'.*

Schefflera actinophylla (umbrella plant). Min 7.5°C(50°F). Bright/partial shade. The common name of this tree results in some confusion with *Heptapleurum* (parasol plant), particularly because it also has 'finger' leaves which radiate from a central stalk. Five or six leaflets are common on young plants, but this number increases to as many as a dozen on mature examples. Unlike the parasol plant, *Schefflera* cannot be coaxed into a bushy and compact shape and it is at its most impressive when 1.5–1.8m (5–6ft) tall.

Scindapsus (devil's ivy). Min 10°C(50°F). Partial shade. *S. aureus* was most awkward to cultivate successfully but recent clones are much easier and make excellent climbers, especially up a moss pole. The plant will tolerate moderate shade but again, as a variegated subject, it needs good light to preserve its leaf colour. Some named varieties and other species do not have such an agreeable disposition, and 'Marble Queen' and *S. pictus* are decidedly difficult to care for.

Tolmiea (piggy-back plant). Min 4.5°C(40°F). Bright/partial shade. *T. menziesii* derives its descriptive nickname from an unusual ability to form juvenile plants at the centre of mature leaves resulting in simple propagation. It is amongst the hardiest of indoor plants and in many districts survives the winter in the garden. Indoors, it forms a compact shape which is equally suited to pots or hanging containers and, if cherished, remains healthy throughout the year. Some plants show pleasantly variegated leaves but this is less likely if placed in a shady place.

Tradescantia Min 7.5°C(45°F). Bright. This genus, which commemorates John Tradescant (the gardener to Charles I), contains three or four species which are highly successful in the house and attract the name of wandering jew or inch plant. Confusingly, the same affectionate titles are used for two similar genera, *Zebrina* and *Callisia*, and it is this kind of complication which puts plant enthusiasts off using popular names.

Fig 26 'Marble Queen' is one of the varieties of Scindapsus which has remarkable foliage, but it does require careful cultivation to maintain it in good condition.

The most usually seen *Tradescantia* is *T. fluminensis* 'Variegata' which is white and green, but there is also a tricolour version in which the leaves are tinged with pink. *T. blossfeldiana* and *T. albovittata* are variations on the theme of striped variegations. Two other genera which are often grouped under the general heading of *Tradescantia* are *Setcreasea purpurea* (purple heart) and *Cyanotis kewensis* (teddy bear vine). All these plants have a trailing habit and are well adapted to house conditions, but note that practically all are variegated and good light is essential to preserve these leaf markings.

Yucca elephantipes (spineless yucca). Min 7.5°C(45°F). Sun/bright. This plant reached its fashionable peak a few years ago but never became very popular perhaps because the price was often high. If the *Yucca* can occupy a really

Fig 27 A forest of Yucca elephantipes enjoying the bright light which is essential for continued growth and good health.

sunny position and is watered frequently, except in winter, it is easy to grow, but perhaps the best policy is to put the plant outdoors over summer. This enables the *Yucca* to take advantage of the maximum available light and it benefits greatly from this treatment. *Y. elephantipes* is the favoured species for home growers because its leaves do not have the dangerous potential of *Y. aloifolia*, which is ominously named Spanish bayonet.

OPEN-ROOM FLOWERING PLANTS

With only a few exceptions common flowering plants are temporary additions to the indoor garden scene. In most cases the initiation of flowering ability requires a higher light level than is usual in living rooms, and plants are either purchased in bloom or cultivated to that stage in a greenhouse or conservatory. It is therefore inevitable that choice is limited to summer-flowering plants which can be accommodated on windowsills, preferably with a southern aspect. As they will only spend a few weeks in the house, the quality of cultivation is not crucial, but proper attention will ensure the maximum period of colourful display.

However, there is a smaller group of plants which are attractive whether in bloom or not, and which need the permanent protection of an indoor environment. Amongst these 'permanents' are some which would be severely stressed by lengthy spells of fierce sunshine. When this occurs a south-facing window is unsuitable (particularly during June, July and August), and a situation must be found where there is little, if any, direct sunlight.

PERMANENT FLOWERERS

Abutilon Min 10°C(50°F). Bright, no sun. *A. striatum* 'Thompsonii' (spotted flowering maple) is the favourite species and its light green

Fig 28 *The variegated* Abutilon *is a lovely bright plant with pendulous flowers which have a long season.* Abutilon *may get tall and 'leggy', but they are not harmed by vigorous pruning.*

leaves, with yellow markings, have a fresh and bright appearance. Orange-red flowers are produced in summer and are enhanced by the translucency of the foliage. *A. megapotamicum* does not have such appealing foliage but it too has yellow variegations and the weeping, lantern-shaped flowers are delightful. Both plants can reach 1.5–1.8m(5–6ft) in height but this can be modified by pruning and, regardless of space limitations, they should be cut down to about 60cm(2ft) each autumn.

Allamanda carthatica (common allamanda). Min 13°C(55°F). Bright/partial shade. A tropical, evergreen climber which can make a very big plant but it will also flower whilst young and small. The flowers are waxy, yellow trumpets and the glossy, dark green foliage gives a good year-round display.

Anthurium scherzerianum (flamingo flower). Min 16°C(60°F). Bright, no summer sun. Beautiful, exotic, waxy flowers with prominent stamens and dark green, spear-shaped leaves

make this a most desirable plant. A reasonable degree of humidity is needed otherwise the foliage may sicken and the flowers may not form. Another species, *A. andreanum*, is much larger with similar flowers but the leaves are heart-shaped and successful cultivation is more difficult.

Aphelandra squarrosa (zebra plant). Min 13°C (55°F). Bright, no summer sun. Despite its succulent appearance this requires moderate humidity and a compost which is kept permanently moist. The yellow cone-shaped flowers last for some weeks; thereafter the white and very prominent leaf veins are an attractive feature.

Begonia Min 13°C(55°F). Bright, no sun. There are many attractive species which will thrive throughout the year if the minimum temperature is observed, and the compost is kept moist but not wet. None of those listed have outstanding flowers but the charm of the *Begonia* is the combination of distinctive foliage and flower clusters, usually pink or red, lasting for many months.

Fig 29   Anthurium andreanum *(painter's palette) is a difficult plant to please but its flowers (technically a spathe and spadix) last for many weeks.*

Fig 30   *The flowers of Aphelandra are curious and colourful over a long period, but the common name of zebra plant clearly refers to the foliage.*

Fig 32 *The shrimp plant is no great beauty but the coloured bracts live for months. Cultivation and propagation are simple.*

Fig 31 Begonia sutherlandii — *one plant will easily fill a 15cm (6in) basket.*

B. argenteo guttata (trout begonia) — upright habit.
B. coccinea (angel wing begonia) — upright.
B. fuchsoides (fuchsia begonia) — bushy.
B. glaucophylla — trailing type.
B. haageana (elephant's ear begonia) — bushy.
B. lucerna (spotted angel wing begonia) — upright.
B. metallica (metal leaf begonia) — bushy.
B. semperflorens (wax begonia) — bushy.
B. serrapetala (pink spot begonia).
B. sutherlandii — bushy with a tendency to trail.

The last named species deserves special mention because its qualities have only recently been recognized and it is becoming widely available. Again, the flowers are not individually impressive but they come in long succession, the plant is able to match its growth to any size container, and the gently trailing foliage is always pretty.

Beloperone guttata (shrimp plant). Min 7.5°C (45°F). Bright, some sun. Some sunshine is necessary to prompt the unusual flower heads which can be present for most of the year, but without them the plant is unremarkable. It is easily grown and as long as it is pruned hard every spring, its habit remains bushy.

Bougainvillea glabra (paper flower). Min 7.5°C (45°F). Sun. Mediterranean coastline visitors will be familiar with this climbing shrub which adorns white-painted walls and delights with its colourful bracts. It can be confined to modest proportions without impairing its flowering ability, and indeed it must be pruned severely in the autumn. If the plant is kept in the brightest part of an unheated room, with a virtually dry compost over winter, it will flower well from late spring and for most of the summer.

Bouvardia domestica (jasmine plant). Min 10°C (50°F). Bright, no summer sun. Quite an uncommon subject but highly desirable for its scented clusters of bloom which appear from late summer until early winter. Pruning is required after the final flowers, and a fairly dry compost is needed until the shrub starts into spring growth.

Bromeliads Min 10°C(50°F). Bright, no sun. This group of plants offers highly decorative foliage and really spectacular flowers, although they usually appear only on mature specimens. Like some orchids many bromeliads grow in tropical trees and are prone to excess water

Fig 33   Undoubtedly happier when it is climbing over Mediterranean walls, Bougainvillea can be confined to a small pot where it can flower well. A few named varieties are offered – this one is 'Alexandra'.

around the roots. When some species have finished flowering the main growth dies and the offsets need to be taken off and planted separately. Watering is unusual for some bromeliads and consists of filling the centre of the growth, which forms a small 'cup'. Those which do not form such a cup should always be watered sparingly, never allowing the compost to become wet. The following list is not exhaustive and contains examples which are commonly grown:

Aechmea fasciata (urn plant) – probably the best-known decorative Bromeliad.
Ananas comosus (pineapple) – spiteful leaves but small fruit may form.
Billbergia nutans (queen's tears) – perhaps the easiest to grow and flower.
Cryptanthus acaulis (green earth star) – compact rosette of leaves.
Guzmania lingulata (scarlet star) – crimson bracts in winter.
Neoregelia carolinae (blushing bromeliad) – base of central leaves turns red.

Fig 34   The bromeliads are frequently grown for their flowers but many have distinguished foliage. This Guzmania is reminiscent of a bushy and compact Aspidistra and will withstand some harsh treatment.

Fig 35   Neoregelia tricolour *is the blushing bromeliad because the basal area of the leaves turns red when the central flower is forming.*

Nidularium innocentii (bird's nest bromeliad) – autumn flowering.
Tillandsia lindenii (blue flowered torch) – narrow leaves, pretty flowers and bracts.
Vriesea splendens (flaming sword) – superb foliage, flower spike in late summer.

Brunfelsia calycina (yesterday, today and tomorrow). Min 10°C(50°F). Bright/shade in summer. An intriguing common name referring to the flower colour which begins purple, becomes paler and finally turns white. The blooms are slightly fragrant and appear almost throughout the year. An agreeably slow-growing evergreen shrub, responsive to light pruning.

Callistemon citrinus (bottle brush plant). Min 7.5°C(45°F). Sun. Its Australian pedigree makes this shrub indifferent to dry air, and the unique flowers compensate for a rather vigorous bush. Plenty of water during the growing season with as much sunshine as possible promotes flowering, and spring pruning will curb its enthusiastic expansion.

Fig 36 A calamondin orange tree with variegated foliage. In the right position it will flower and produce small but useable fruit.

Campanula isophylla (star of Bethlehem). Min 7.5°C(45°F). Bright, some sun. A long-flowering subject at its best as a hanging plant, and when kept cool. White, blue and lilac varieties are easily grown from seed but it is a slow job, whereas cuttings are quickly rooted.

Citrus mitis (calamondin orange). Min 10°C (50°F). Sunny/bright. Oranges and lemons will succeed in the home but indifferent results are achieved from pips, so it is preferable to cultivate those with a known pedigree. *C. mitis* is ideal, producing flowers and colourful fruit for much of the year on a compact bush, but most other *Citrus* trees grow quite large before fruiting.

Clerodendrum thomsonae (glory bower). Min 13°C(55°F). Bright, no sun. Although quite a strong climber it can be restricted by pruning. Will only remain healthy in humid surroundings and must be watered very sparingly over winter.

Fig 37 The choice blooms of Clivia miniata are worth waiting for, but the cultural requirements must be met if this is to be an annual event.

Clivia miniata (Kaffir lily). Min 4.5°C(40°F). Bright, no sun. Looking rather like an aristocratic leek, *Clivia's* dark green leaves are always distinguished; the spring or early summer flowers, in red or orange, are really magnificent. A cool winter is needed with minimal water, but otherwise the plant is very tolerant and lives for many years producing offspring as it matures.

Columnea banksii (goldfish plant). Min 10°C (50°F). Bright, no summer sun. A number of *Columnea* make colourful hanging subjects with their tubular flowers but *C. banksii*, because of its waxy leaves, is probably one of the easiest to grow without extra humidity.

Crossandra undulifolia (firecracker flower). Min 13°C(55°F). Bright, no sun. A quite beautiful subject which starts flowering whilst very small and is often colourful from spring until autumn. The leaves are glossy and much admired but the plant does have a drawback — it must be grown in a

Fig 38 Delicate Episcia *need the refuge of a humid enclosure such as the plastic dome illustrated. Not only is it ideal for small plants, it can also be used as a propagator and to create extra humidity; the hole can be covered with cling film.*

gravel tray to provide the envelope of moist air which is essential for healthy growth.

Cuphea ignea (cigar plant). Min 13°C(55°F). Bright, some sun. The curious flowers and robust nature make *Cuphea* an easy plant to care for, but it has no special charm and becomes straggly with age.

Dipladenia sanderi (pink allamanda). Min 13°C (50°F). Bright, no sun. A natural climber responsive to pruning which is necessary to preserve a bushy shape. The flowers are pink and trumpet-shaped appearing from June to September, but extra humidity should be provided.

Episcia cupreata (flame violet). Min 16°C(60°F). Bright, no sun. This member of the Gesneriad family is one of the delights of the plant world — it has glorious silver and green leaves with an attractive textured surface. The brilliant red flowers appear in early summer. Warmth is vital for *Episcia* so it is worth keeping them over winter in a heated propagator. High humidity is also a prerequisite for really healthy growth.

Euphorbia milii (splendens) (crown of thorns). Min 13°C(55°F). Bright, some sun. A very resilient, noble plant with eye-catching deep red bracts and scarlet stems. However, the plant has vicious thorns, the sap is poisonous, and growth is recklessly untidy. Another species, *E. fulgens* (scarlet plume), is uncommon and has graceful foliage with winter flowers.

Hibiscus rosa-sinensis (rose of China). Min 10°C (50°F). Sun/bright. With permanently moist compost, occasional summer feeding and a sunny position, *Hibiscus* is a showy and long-lived bush. It grows quite large if repotted annually, but pruning and confining to a small pot will make it more manageable. The blooms only last for a day but well-grown plants will provide a long succession of beautiful flowers and the glossy, neat leaves enhance the display. There are an increasing number of varieties available in colours

Fig 39   This named variety of Hibiscus *is 'Tivoli'. The glorious blooms only live for a day but are regularly replaced.*

ranging from white and yellow, to pink, red and orange. Maximum winter light is necessary and in summer a sunny (but never scorching) position is suitable.

Hoya carnosa   (wax plant). Min 10°C(50°F). Bright, some sun. A popular climbing plant with quite fragrant, waxy flower clusters which appear during the summer. *Hoya* is usually trained on a wire ring but, whatever aid is used, some means of support is essential. There is a miniature version, *H. bella*, but it is not so adaptable to room conditions.

Hypocyrta glabra   (clog plant). Min 10°C(50°F). Bright/partial shade. A bushy subject with arching stems clothed in small, succulent leaves; in summer it is covered in masses of orange flowers. A cool, bright room is needed for winter resting and the plant definitely does better in moist air.

Kalanchoe blossfeldiana (flaming Katy). Min 10°C(50°F). Partial shade. Various varieties are sold with yellow or orange flowers, but red is the most common colour. They revel in a dry atmosphere and their foliage is always attractive making them highly versatile as indoor decoration. After flowering remove the spent heads and stems, keep the compost almost dry for a month or so, and then resume normal watering. This technique will usually mean that *Kalanchoe* is in bloom more often than not.

Lantana camara (shrub verbena). Min 10°C (50°F). Bright, some sun. The species has attractive flowerheads which change colour as they age giving the impression of a multi-coloured bush (the heads consist of tiny florets which drop and need a lot of sweeping up). There are also white and yellow forms available but they do not change colour. By nature *Lantana* is quite a large shrub, frequently seen around the Mediterranean, but if the plants are confined to small pots the result is a compact and long-flowering subject.

Pachystachys lutea   (lollipop plant). Min 13°C (55°F). Bright. Similar flowerheads to the shrimp plant, except that they are yellow and erect. These heads are also bracts or modified leaves, the 'real' flowers being white. Cultivation is easy but requires cutting down in the autumn to encourage compact growth the following year.

Passiflora caerulea   (passion flower). Min 7.5°C (45°F). Bright, some sun. A quick-growing vine which is probably best in a greenhouse or conservatory, though it can be successful indoors if allowed to become potbound. It should have a compulsory rest in the winter by being kept in an unheated room, and pruning must be severe in early spring. The complex flowers are fascinating and short-lived, but they are produced in rapid succession in the summer and may be followed by yellow fruits.

35

Fig 40   *The complicated and unique structure of the passion flower; this variety is* P. violacea *'Empress'.*

Pentas lanceolata (Egyptian star cluster). Min 10°C(50°F). Bright, some sun. Still a fairly uncommon plant but gradually becoming more available. Has a welcome habit of flowering at various times of the year and, although the species has pink blooms, there are hybrids in white, red or purple. The flower umbels appear at the tips of the shoots and, if pinched out when 7.5–10cm (3–4in) high, more shoots and flower clusters result. Since the growth habit is rather lax, pinching out the tips keeps the plant in better shape.

Plumbago capensis (Cape leadwort). Min 7.5°C (45°F). Bright, some sun. Produces abundant flowers in a beautiful shade of blue, but the shrub is annoyingly vigorous and its shape is not especially endearing. However, for such a plentiful supply of bloom, such a sacrifice is worth

Fig 4I   Pentas *is a well behaved flowering shrub which blooms whilst it is quite small. It is easily restricted to a modest size by pruning.*

Fig 42 Close-up of the Pentas *flower.*

making – in this case it requires a sustained attack with secateurs after the shrub has overwintered in a cool room.

Punica granatum 'Nana' (pomegranate). Min 7.5°C(45°F). Sun. This miniature pomegranate makes a fine indoor tree which can be trained as a standard or allowed to become more shrub-like. In either case it will not grow higher than about 45cm(18in) and will bear large bell-shaped red flowers, followed by small orange-yellow fruits which are not edible. A cooler, drier rest period is needed in winter.

Ruellia mackoyana Min 13°C(55°F). Bright, some sun. Surprisingly, this easily cultivated and most attractive plant is rarely seen but it is desirable for the dark green leaves which have distinctively marked central veins. The colours of the flowers are pink or red, and highly welcome for their late autumn and winter appearance.

Saintpaulia (African violet). Min 13°C(55°F). Bright, no sun. Compact, pretty, and with a number of different flower colours and forms, the

African violet is rightly the favourite long- term flowering subject for the home. The plants are happiest in humid surroundings but are un-doubtedly able to cope with fairly dry air and the blooms appear at various times of the year. Winter flowers are most likely in the brightest spot (particularly given winter sunshine), and they are also stimulated by ordinary artificial lighting.

Schizocentron elegans (Spanish shawl). Min 13°C(55°F). Bright, some sun. This makes an ex-cellent small plant with dark, hairy leaves and mauve flowers which are evident in late winter and spring. The plant will bloom more profusely if it is grown in a small container and allowed to become potbound, ensuring that the compost is always moist.

Fig 43 Spathyphyllum 'Mauna Loa' (peace lily) has the common name of white sails, which refers to the structure of the flower. Shade and humidity are the plant's main requirements.

Spathiphyllum wallisii (peace lily). Min 13°C (55°F). Bright, some sun. Glossy, spear-shaped leaves make this a graceful plant and the appearance of white, spathe flowers which look rather like arum lilies, is a considerable bonus. However, note that very dry air and strong sunlight will soon ruin the plant's composure and appearance.

Stephanotis floribunda (Madagascar jasmine). Min 13°C(55°F). Bright, some sun. The strongly scented blooms are greatly appreciated but the plant can be awkward to cultivate and reacts badly to large temperature changes. As a climbing plant it needs some means of support as well as a couple of months' rest, at the minimum temperature over winter. When the flower buds

Fig 44 A plant with flowers which are heavily scented and highly prized, but Stephanotis *can be temperamental and should be kept where temperatures are fairly constant.*

form it is important to keep the plant in the same position – if moved, the buds will drop.

Streptocarpus (Cape primrose). Min 10°C (50°F). Bright, no sun. Many hybrids exist with quite a good colour range. The trumpet-shaped flowers are attractively veined and the throats are often in a contrasting shade. Young plants are best because older specimens usually develop large, coarse leaves which are out of scale with the blooms. The plant is easy to care for and will flower for at least half of the year, especially if it is repotted annually and given a few winter weeks with reduced watering.

Vallota speciosa (Scarborough lily). Min 10°C (50°F). Bright, some sun. Red flowers typify the species, but there are varieties which are white or pink and all are very beautiful. The bulbs are quite expensive but the offsets should develop into a healthy clump in a few years, making an impressive display.

TEMPORARY FLOWERERS

There are literally hundreds of plants which flower temporarily in the home. Many are then discarded but others can be saved, in one form or another, for future years. The following list is a selection of suitable subjects which are either highly recommended or fairly unusual. Minimum temperatures are noted when crucial.

Achimenes (hot water plant). Min 16°C(60°F). Full sun. There are dozens of named varieties and hybrids which are fairly easy to cultivate, and whose uncomplicated blooms and luxuriant foliage should not be missed. They grow from small tubers which survive the winter in a cool, dry state; the only nuisance is that they require a temperature above 16°C(60°F) before they will start into growth. If a propagator is unavailable the airing cupboard will suffice. The plants must be moved to a light, warm place as soon as shoots appear.

Fig 45   *White* Catharanthus *with a crimson 'eye', and a pink flowering* Begonia semperflorens *will both do well in bright shade. Direct sun is not required though small amounts will not be harmful.*

Fig 46   *Elatior begonias have become one of the most popular flowering plants; the colours are bright and the plants are trouble-free.*

Azalea indica   (Indian azalea). Bright, no sun. An evergreen plant, frequently given as a Christmas present, which all too often is dead by Easter. Yet there is no reason why *Azalea* should not last for decades. They must have permanently moist lime-free compost. After spending the summer and early autumn outside in a shady spot the plants must be taken indoors, but it is essential they are kept in a cool room. Warm, dry conditions will dessicate the foliage and stimulate early flowering. As lime-haters, hard water is resented and rainwater is preferable.

Begonia   Bright, no sun. The Reiger *Begonia* and, more recently, the Elatiors are superb plants which flower incessantly. Their foliage is an added attraction which stays healthy as long as there is no exposure to strong sunshine. *Begonia semperflorens*, the famous bedding plant, also blooms indefinitely and will tolerate some dryness and sunshine; it can remain in flower over winter if reasonably warm. Admirers of exhibition *Begonia* note that they should not be

39

Fig 47 Catharanthus *(Madagascar periwinkle) has the appearance of a busy Lizzie, but the foliage is much more distinguished.*

grown outside a conservatory or greenhouse; the plants stay reasonably healthy but dry air causes serious bud drop.

Browallia (bush violet). Bright, some sun. Although usually bought in flower, the bush violet can be raised from seed at home. Its blue flowers with white throats are highly decorative, although there are now new hybrids with other colours. A cool room suits it best and regular pinching out of the growing tips will lead to compact growth and a profusion of flowers. (Seed can be sown in the summer for winter-flowering plants, but success is not assured.)

Catharanthus (Madagascar periwinkle). Bright, no sun. Often called *Vinca* in the catalogues, this plant can be grown from seed, producing similar flowers to the busy Lizzie but with more notable foliage. A small amount of sunshine is not harmful

Fig 48 Celosia plumosa *(Prince of Wales' feathers) with a variegated* Euonymus.

40

Fig 49   Pot-mums are a popular flowering pot plant. They last well in cool conditions and the range of colours is very pleasing.

but *Catharanthus* blooms well over a long period if kept in comparative shade.

Celosia   Sun. *C. cristata* (cockscomb) and *C. plumosa* (Prince of Wales' feathers) are both showy summer plants. The flowerheads are unusual and vividly coloured, and the dwarf forms are convenient for a sunny windowsill.

Chrysanthemum   Bright, no sun. Flowers over a long period if kept cool in a bright place. Forced cultivation and chemicals ensure that compact plants are sold all year round, but beware taking cuttings. They root very easily but the plants will grow at least 45cm(18in) tall.

Cyclamen persicum   (shooting star). Bright, no sun. Another Christmas favourite which struggles to survive in centrally-heated rooms, and usually fails. It is intolerant of temperatures in excess of

16°C(60°F), otherwise the corm will survive for some years. However, it is unlikely that subsequent years will see a performance to match the first.

Erica   (heather). Bright, some sun. *E. gracilis* (Christmas heather) and *E. hyemalis* (Cape heath) are perhaps the only two heathers seen indoors, though neither will be seen for long in high temperatures. Kept cool or even cold, and in a light position, they will give pleasure for some weeks; rainwater is preferable in hard-water districts.

Euphorbia pulcherrima   (poinsettia).   Bright, some sun. Brilliantly coloured bracts and pleasant foliage make this an attractive Christmas present. It will remain attractive for many weeks if the temperature is held below 21°C(70°F). Few gardeners will bother inducing flowers for the

41

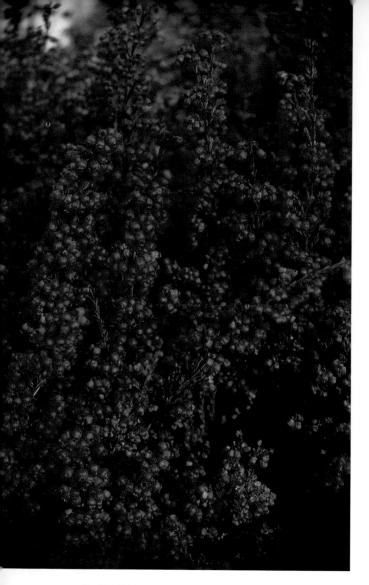

Fig 50 Erica gracilis *can give a brilliant and long-lasting show, but if it is not kept really cool it will not justify its name of Christmas heather.*

following season, but it is interesting to try. The plants need cutting back to 7.5–10cm(3–4in) high and repotting in late spring; thereafter cultivation is simple. However, from the end of September until the first days of December, poinsettias must be kept in the dark for 14 hours each day, otherwise flowering will occur long after Christmas.

Eustoma grandiflora (prairie gentian). Sun. Some catalogues use the name *Lisianthus russelianus* for this plant which is too tall for a windowsill, but the flowers are magnificent and

each lasts over a fortnight. Only purple, white or pink blooms are possible but the flower form changes as it ages; initially tight petals like a tulip but subsequently resembling a poppy. Propagation from seed is trouble-free, but the young plants grow slowly. The plants resent undue root disturbance.

Exacum affine (Persian violet). Bright, some sun. A compact plant with pretty, glossy foliage and masses of tiny, pink or blue flowers which are slightly fragrant. It is easily grown from seed.

Fuchsia (lady's eardrops). Bright, no sun. Greatly admired flowers but imperfect plants in the home, resenting the dry atmosphere. They also dislike high temperatures, the plants are amongst the first to wilt under heat or indeed water stress.

Gloxinia speciosa Bright, no sun. More accurately called *Sinningia*, these plants are usually bought in flower but can simply be grown from tubers which are potted up in the spring. However, they are difficult to maintain indoors because of the humidity requirement – the use of a pebble tray is a definite prerequisite for success.

Heliotropium hybrida (cherry pie). Bright, some sun. Clusters of purple florets (quite fragrant) and sculptured-looking leaves with prominent veining are the plant's hallmarks. Formerly a regular in summer bedding schemes, it is now almost a rarity and deserves a second chance as a houseplant. It can be sustained for a few years but new plants are easy to raise from either cuttings or seed, and it is not worthwhile keeping old specimens.

Hippeastrum hybrida (amaryllis). Bright, some sun. Although the flowering period is quite short, *Hippeastrum* has become one of the most popular houseplants because the giant blooms are so impressive. It is normally bought as a bulb and the first flowers are virtually guaranteed, but

Fig 51   The most lovely and long-lasting flowers of Eustoma – in purple, white and mauve. They are equally at home on a sunny windowsill or in a greenhouse.

Fig 52   The hybrid Gloxinia are highly desirable subjects, but dry air causes the foliage to lose its lustre and the flower buds to drop.

some difficulty can be experienced in achieving a repeat performance. When the petals have fallen, the seed heads should be removed and the plant must be maintained by watering and occasional feeding until the leaves begin to wither and die. The bulb needs a frost-free and dry situation for a few weeks, when it can be moved to a warmer place. Water should be withheld until the first signs of new growth are visible and the compost should only be barely moist until the flower bud emerges.

Hydrangea macrophylla   Bright, no sun. Once a great favourite, it has become another casualty of the central-heating age because it ails rapidly at temperatures of over 18.5°C(65°F). If treated to a cool, bright regime it will delight for years, and only needs the stems to be shortened after flowering and then repotting. It can spend the summer and autumn outdoors.

Impatiens   (busy Lizzie). Bright, no sun. The modern examples of this genus are very different from the old specimens which became gaunt and leafless as they tenaciously clung to life in living-rooms all over the country. Long, fleshy and ugly stems surmounted by occasional flowers have been replaced by compact, bushy plants which bloom ceaselessly and in an unparalleled colour range. They do equally well in the home and garden bedding schemes, but they do not relish scorching sunshine, nor do they enjoy dry compost. The so-called New Guinea hybrids are now widely sold, and grow taller but have distinguished and sometimes variegated leaves. All are easily kept over winter in a bright and reasonably warm place; cut them down in the spring and repot.

Lachenalia aloides   (Cape cowslip). Bright, some sun. Groups of pendant flowers, yellow tinged

Fig 53   Elatior begonias and regal pelargoniums will flower for months in a bright situation, even if there is very little sunshine.

with red and green, and leaves which have blotches in various shades of brown. Such a description suggests everyone would like to grow this bulbous plant but it has such a record of failure in the home that it is rarely seen. Central heating is again the villain because the Cape cowslip fades away at any hint of winter heat. It flowers between December and March and needs a cold room. If watering is continued until June and then stopped completely until September, the bulbs will be ready for an encore.

Pelargonium (geranium). Sun, bright. The ordinary geranium, *P. zonale*, is an uneasy occupant of even the sunniest windowsill because it is a subject for maximum light levels. However the regal varieties, *P. domesticum*, do not require direct sunshine in any quantity and there are many named varieties which offer spectacular and protracted flowering. The ivy-leaf types, *P. peltatum*, are resilient but a position in maximum light and sunshine is imperative.

Primula (primrose). Bright, no sun. Wonderfully cheerful plants which are most welcome in winter and spring, but they will deteriorate rapidly at temperatures above 16°C(60°F). If you must keep one in a warm living-room then provide a gravel tray. There are now innumerable

Fig 54 'Mrs Henry Cox' is a famous name amongst zonal geraniums. When grown indoors it needs maximum light and sunshine to flower well, and to bring out the striking foliage colours.

Fig 55 The flowers of the ivy leaf geranium 'Rouletta' or 'Mexicana'.

Fig 56   *The flowers of* Primula obconica *become paler as they age; this plant is called the poison primula although the worst it can do is give someone a skin rash.*

Fig 57   *Close up of* Torenia *blooms showing the similarity to foxgloves.*

strains of primrose, but the old reliable kinds are still available – *P. malacoides*, *P. sinensis*, *P. kewensis* and *P. obconica*. The latter comes in superb colours, but note that some people are allergic to it.

Salpiglossis sinuata (painted tongue). Sun. Usually a disappointing subject for summer bedding but as a pot plant it is able to show off its gorgeous flowers to best advantage. It is a somewhat untidy grower and a few small sticks may be needed for support, but all will be forgiven when you see the exquisite blooms, marbled and veined in contrasting colours.

Schizanthus pinnatus (poor man's orchid). Bright, some sun. The markings on the petals are almost as exotic as those of *Salpiglossis* and the plant is equally easy to grow. Many different colours are available from various strains of seed but all have pretty, ferny foliage and can be grown both for spring and summer display. Growing shoots should be pinched out regularly whilst young, so that the plant is floriferous and compact.

Sprekelia formosissima (jacobean lily). Sun. Flowering dependably, year after year, this bulbous plant has deep crimson blooms in summer which can only be described as having classic simplicity. The compost should be almost dry

46

Fig 58 The Aster 'Pinocchio' makes a superb bedding plant, but its small
size is such that it can also be a reasonably compact pot plant.

over winter and the bulbs need to be repotted before spring. At this time there will almost certainly be a few juvenile bulbs which have formed next to the 'mother', and they can be potted separately.

Thunbergia alata (black-eyed Susan). Bright, some sun. A quick-growing climber which can be raised as a supported pot plant or placed in a hanging container. The characteristic flowers, usually orange or yellow, have a dark 'eye' and the foliage is pleasant. It is possible to keep

Fig 59   The 'Lime Green' variety of Nicotiana domino is an example of a bedding subject which makes an excellent pot plant. It is very easy to grow from seed.

Thunbergia for the following year, but the plants are so easy to grow from seed it is hardly worthwhile.

Torenia   Bright, some sun. An outstanding flowering plant known to very few but deserving a place on every windowsill. A bright place with some sunshine will give innumerable flowers in pink, white or shades of blue, often bi-coloured and reminiscent of miniature foxgloves.

I should repeat that this list of temporary flowering subjects is merely a selection from hundreds of candidates, and many perfectly delightful plants have been excluded on account of their size. *Agapanthus* — with its 90cm(3ft) flower stems — is one example and it really needs to be grown in a tub. I also regret excluding *Strelitzia* (bird of paradise flower), because it is arguably the most exciting flower of all, but this too grows 90–120cm(3–4ft) high and needs at least a 25cm(10in) pot. In addition it will not flower until it is five to six years old.

Busy Lizzie and *Begonia semperflorens* have been mentioned as outstanding representatives of those plants which serve us so well as summer bedding, but there are many others which are superb as indoor flowering subjects. It is a good idea when buying bedding plants to use a few for pots; the prospects for a colourful windowsill are assured because most of the small varieties give excellent results. A good compost is desirable and as the flowers will not be damaged by wind and rain, they can reveal their full potential. A full list would run into pages, but you will not be disappointed by the following: *Ageratum*, *Anchusa*, *Antirrhinum*, *Aster*, *Gazania*, *Lobelia*, *Calendula* (French and dwarf African), *Nicotiana*, *Petunia*, *Salvia*, *Verbena*, and *Zinnia*. I must emphasize that where bedding plants are being grown for home decoration the sunniest spot available will bring the best results, but bear in mind that relentless days of scorching sunshine will put most plants under stress. For those subjects which are described as greenhouse varieties, you must ascertain whether or not they are suited to prolonged exposure to sunshine.

If you are one of the hundreds of gardeners who grow their own plants from seed you have an excellent choice. Not only is there now an increased range of garden plants, but also the option of raising greenhouse and houseplants which are eminently suited to windowsill life. The best course of action is to obtain one of the comprehensive seed catalogues, and spend time browsing through their listings. Information is given about the ultimate height of the subject,

germination temperature, and the best time of year to sow. If you are adventurous much of the fascinating plant life of the planet is at your fingertips, and with commonsense and enthusiasm they can be raised in the home. Please don't be deterred by unfamiliar names – in fact make a point of trying plants of which you have never heard. Therein lies the real element of discovery and excitement.

OTHER INTERESTING PLANTS
Cacti and Succulents

For open-room placings there are hundreds of cacti and succulents which will thrive in sunny spots, totally unaffected by dry air. They are, however, rather specialized in their appeal and many people feel that they look out of place (especially the desert cacti) beside the more conventional houseplants. Nonetheless, a few succulents have been mentioned in previous categories and a couple more should not be ignored.

Aloe variegata looks like a small, fan-shaped *Sanseveiria* and its common name, partridge breast, is apt. *Agave americana* 'Mediopicta' has saw-edged leaves with a white central band. Two of the forest cacti, which are often believed to be succulents, are *Zygocactus truncatus* (Christmas cactus), and *Schlumbergera gaertneri* (Easter cactus). These two look woefully bare when not in flower but there is compensation in colourful displays which occur at drab times of the year. This is also true of the many *Epiphyllum* hybrids which are ugly plants but the flowers, though ephemeral, are really magnificent.

For anyone who finds succulents and cacti irresistible, the real recipe for success is maximum light at all times while ensuring that the plants are cold and dry over winter. Cold does not mean below freezing point, but temperatures which are near to that will do no harm as long as the compost is dry – and that means *no* water from November to March. This apparently harsh treatment will call for the utmost self-discipline on the part of the cultivator, but it is one of

Fig 60 *A very neat, compact succulent,* Aloe variegata *(partridge breast), which will survive indefinitely providing the watering can is allowed to gather dust in winter.*

Fig 61 Schlumbergera truncata, *or* Zygocactus truncatus, *the Christmas cactus.*

the secrets of prompting many cacti to bloom in the spring.

Bonsai

Bonsai is rarely discussed in books on house-plants because the trees and shrubs tradition-ally used for miniaturization were hardy. It was imperative that the plants were grown outdoors and only brought inside for short periods other-wise they suffered greatly from the effects of heat and lack of humidity. However, in recent years there has been a move towards using semi-tropical species which are much more likely to succeed indoors, although they should still spend some time outside when the weather is suit-able.

The essence of bonsai is to produce a miniature version of mature specimens, and the most desirable feature is that it should look an-cient, rugged, gnarled and weather-beaten. There are many different styles recognized by devotees and most require a degree of training and usually the help of wire. The plant is kept small by pruning both the roots and the top growth, and confining it in a small, shallow con-tainer. There is a mistaken belief that bonsai plants must be starved to keep them from grow-ing but nothing is further from the truth. They should be fed regularly whilst growing so that the trunk and selected branches will thicken and give the appearance of maturity as soon as possible.

Bonsai cultivation presents few problems but it must be appreciated that pruning and repotting will be necessary throughout the plant's life. Also, since they are kept permanently in small pots, the water requirements will be high. Those which can spend most of the time indoors are

Fig 62 Ulmus parvifola *(Chinese elm) is a semi-evergreen which can tolerate the fluctuating conditions in the house and is a superb subject for bonsai. The specimen shown is a 15-year-old tree.*

especially prone to dehydration, and in summer a twice-daily watering may be required.

Training a bonsai from the seedling stage is an intriguing pursuit and financially sensible because established examples can be very expensive.

Any of the following suggestions of indoor bonsai could be used in a miniature garden or in a terrarium, but remember that bonsai must remain in their pots or they will not remain small.

Chamaecyparis pisifera 'Squarrosa' (moss cypress) – one of very few cypresses for indoors.
Crassula argentea (jade plant) – very suitable plant for bonsai treatment.
Ficus benjamina (weeping fig) – as listed elsewhere, a beautiful plant.
Pinus pinea (stone pine) – the most suitable pine for indoor bonsai.
Punica granatum 'Nana' (dwarf pomegranate) – will flower and fruit as a bonsai.
Ulmus parvifola (Chinese elm) – an attractive tree which develops quite quickly.

And finally, if you buy a bonsai remember to make sure that you know whether it is suitable for indoors or outdoors.

Fig 63   The variegated weeping fig is a graceful and versatile plant which is eminently suited to bonsai treatment. Even the two-year-old example on the left is beginning to show signs of maturity; the other one is four years old.

CHAPTER 3

Gardens Behind Glass

BOTTLES

There is no doubt that plants gain an extra dimension when viewed behind glass, and there are numerous containers perfectly suited for this purpose. Terraria and plant cases are specially constructed for house plants and are dealt with later, however, the cheapest glass vessel, which comes in a variety of shapes and sizes is the bottle.

Glass bottles are not as common as they were and they have been largely replaced by plastic containers, which are not ideal as bottle gardens. Plants will grow admirably in plastic bottles as long as they are transparent, but the material is soft and easily scratched, lacks charm, and whereas condensation runs down glass, it 'sticks' to plastic. Any glass container will suffice as long as it is large enough to house one or more plants, and has an adequately sized opening to facilitate the planting. Carboys, which were mostly used to transport acids and other corrosive liquids, are no longer commonly available, and many people might now consider them to be too large and obtrusive for the modern home. Smaller carboys are made especially or gardeners and are widely available, some being made of clear glass, others in shades of green. The former are best because inside they are obviously brighter, although those with a slightly green cast are undoubtedly attractive.

Alternatives to the traditional bottles and carboys include goldfish bowls, sweet jars, and wide-necked decanters. Large ornamental brandy glasses will look very distinctive when planted with a single specimen, and if you are willing to make some slight modification to bell-jars and glass cheese covers they are ideal, informal plant cases. With a little imagination and several visits to antique and bric-a-brac shops you will certainly encounter a wide range of jars and vases which will add a touch of originality to your plant display.

One of the joys of bottle gardens is that, with the exception of the carboys, they are easily moved from place to place and the smaller containers can be used to decorate the dinner table for a special occasion. Otherwise, they can be moved around the home taking advantage of the best light in summer and winter. Such versatility is fun, and combines with an element of novelty,

Fig 64 A large bottle (or small carboy) bursting with vegetation. In a few months it will have to be emptied and replanted.

Fig 65   Large and small pear-shaped bottles, with one small spherical version. Note that all have useful side-planting holes.

but do not forget that the main feature of bottle gardening is that it enables you to succeed with 'difficult' plants. The usual problems of low humidity and lethal cold draughts are immediately avoided. Damaging influences are banished.

If the bottle top is kept open there will be some loss of moisture, but the humidity will nevertheless be high; if a stopper is used the interior becomes a self-contained environment in which oxygen and carbon dioxide are recycled, and water vapour condenses on the glass, running back into the compost for re-use. In fact the main danger with this form of gardening is success, and overplanted containers will soon suffer overcrowding when the full potential of the plants is liberated by these ideal conditions.

Bottles and jars which are sufficiently large to admit a hand are easy to plant, but when the neck is narrow special implements are needed

Fig 66 (left)   A wrought-iron stand has both a practical purpose and adds to the decorative value of a bottle containing Pilea, Ficus pumila, and Selaginella.

Fig 67   A new breed of bottle especially made for plants, with the
convenience of a hand-size opening at the side.

Fig 68 A pear-shaped bottle, showing
Dracaena sanderiana, Syngonium, and a
flaming Katy.

Fig 69 A pear-shaped bottle, again with a
plant hole in the side, which contains ivy, a
polka-dot plant, and a red flowering
Kalanchoe.

for planting and subsequent maintenance. Tools
for the purpose can be purchased or improvized,
using everyday kitchen utensils. A fork and
spoon, both tied to slim canes of the appropriate
length, become fork and spade, and a similar
cane with a razor blade embedded in the end
becomes a pruning device for trimming growth
or cutting off dead leaves. Removal of the debris
is achieved by a cane-mounted needle, or you
can make a more sophisticated extractor based
on the principle of a clothes peg. One final and
vital implement is a small piece of sponge attached to stiff wire which will enable you to clean the
inside of the glass.

Preparation

First wash the bottle outside and in. Then insert
2.5cm(1in) of washed or pea gravel to cover the
base, followed by a similar depth of charcoal. This
crucial initial filling provides drainage, absorbs
gases, and helps prevent the rooting medium
from becoming stagnant. Horticultural charcoal
seems to be unobtainable these days, but the
kind used for barbecues is entirely satisfactory
(small pieces are needed; the larger ones are
easily broken up). Next insert peat-based,
reasonably dry compost to a depth of about
7.5cm (3in), or slightly less for a small bottle. All
the materials mentioned so far can be poured

Fig 70   A globular bottle with a hole in the side revealing Hypoestes *and* Syngonium.

Fig 71   Another globular bottle with an excellent variety of foliage shape and colour.

into the bottle using a funnel or cardboard tube, although a suitable substitute can be made by folding fairly stiff paper.

Planting

Putting the plants into narrow-necked bottles can be tricky. The emphasis is more on patience and determination than dexterity and skill, and provided the roots are covered by compost all will be well. It may take time to achieve the desired planting arrangement, but persevere. If the bottle can accommodate only one plant the subject looks better in the centre, but if inserting three or four you must decide if your display will be viewed from one side only. Taller plants must then be to the rear whereas if the bottle will be viewed from all sides, place the tallest plant in the centre.

57

Fig 72   A typical selection of young houseplants offered by many garden centres. They are essential for terrarium and bottle planting, and much cheaper than mature specimens.

Watering

The first piece of advice is do not overdo it or it will take a long time for the excess to evaporate through the narrow opening. The safest method is to use a small hand spray and err on the dry side, knowing that more can be added. You will soon see over the first few days whether the correct amount of water has been added – the plants will not be wilting and there will only be a small amount of condensation on the inside of the bottle, usually in the mornings. The same precautions must be taken if the bottle top is to be closed, and although in this case morning condensation may be greater, it should still clear as the day progresses.

Siting

Since the bottle plants are safe from draughts and benefit from a humid atmosphere, there are only two factors for consideration – temperature and light. Both will depend on where the bottle is sited. Provided all the plants have similar requirements the only possible conflict is between their needs and where you think the container looks best. The fact that this is a mobile garden gives ample opportunity for compromise. However, it should never be in a position of full sun during the summer otherwise barbecued vegetation will result, although winter sunshine is welcome and harmless.

Temperature will not be a difficulty in centrally-heated homes, but it should be borne in mind that the majority of plants prefer an even warmth without large fluctuations. Spring,

Fig 73   Winter sunshine marking out the light zones in a living room.

Fig 74   Winter sunshine illuminates the bottle and gives useful, extra light, but glass enclosures should never be exposed to summer sunshine.

summer and autumn will not stress your plants, but winter is a time when they will survive rather than flourish, and they need as much help as they can get.

Maintenance

You should find that maintenance is minimal and I believe that enclosure gardening will give the best chance of a prolonged and trouble-free display. You may need to remove the occasional leaf before it decays and it may just be necessary to add a small amount of water (if the moisture content of the compost was roughly correct at the time of planting, even with an open-topped bottle, that should be an end to it). And finally it is a sound idea to note the colour of the compost when it is dry *and* moist because this will be an excellent future guide.

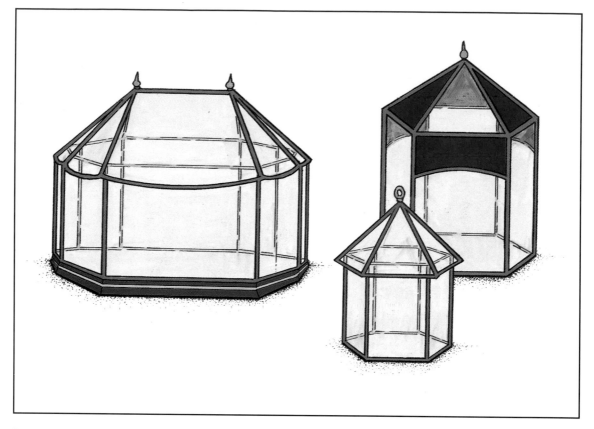

Fig 75   A selection of small and large terraria in the leaded glass style.

Fig 76   A leaded glass terrarium with the added distinction of a wooden base and the convenience of a removable roof.

Do's and Don'ts

Do use small plants.
Do check the plants regularly.
Do ensure that plants are pest-free.
Do remove dead flowers, leaves and stems.
Don't overcrowd the bottle.
Don't water excessively.
Don't put the bottle in direct sunshine.
Don't expect an eternal display.

TERRARIA AND PLANT CASES

The fashion for growing plants in closed cases probably began in America in the late 1930s. The word terrarium was used quite widely but the term has changed significantly. Now it embraces the modern glass structures which might be circular, triangular or rectangular or indeed any shape at all, and the variety of styles is numerous.

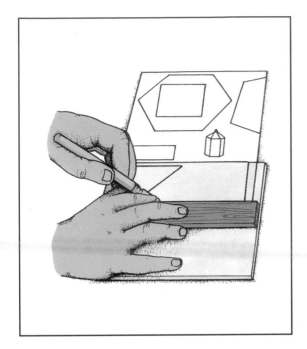

Fig 77 Terrarium glass being cut over a printed 'pattern' with a wheeled cutter.

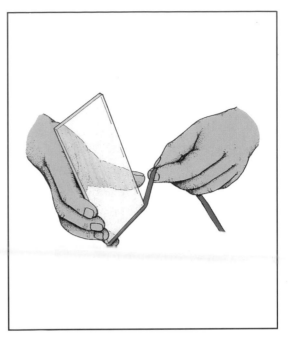

Fig 78 All the edges are then 'taped' with self-adhesive copper strip.

Fig 79 Two sets of glass, cut to size with an assembled, small terrarium.

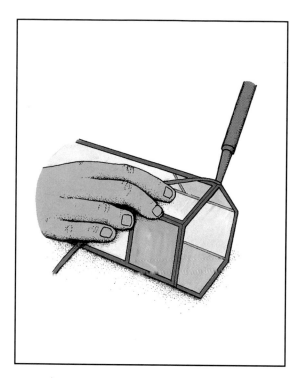

Fig 80   The glass sections are secured by soldering the copper strips together.

In fact the word terrarium is not that important because the simplest, most practical and cheapest examples are what people would call an aquarium.

Usually they are made only from toughened glass, although older designs are framed with metal, often an aluminium alloy which does not rust. They tend to be high in relation to their length, and consequently give ample headroom for a wide range of plants. Various sizes and fitted canopies are available which can accommodate some means of lighting, or simply for enclosing the aquarium. When purchasing a terrarium remember that they can be bought second hand. What may have been manufactured as a fish tank will make a superb home for plants, and although they may not look right everywhere in the home I do think that the frameless examples are perfectly acceptable.

Those terraria which have been specifically designed as interior ornaments come in a variety of shapes, although most seem to be in a Victorian style, and often more attractive than functional. The glass panels, sometimes stained, are invariably leaded; another common feature is unglazed sections allowing trailing plants to spill out in a most natural manner. It is also possible to buy a modern recreation which has a ring in the top of the frame, giving the option of a suspended terrarium. In other words the choice of plant containers is wide enough, I believe, for even the most discerning home gardener to find one which is pleasing in style and sufficiently practical to afford useful protection for plants.

Those of a more adventurous disposition may like the idea of constructing a terrarium, and will find kits on sale containing all the necessary items including glass cut to size. The more ambitious could even design and construct their own terrarium from basic materials, tailoring the style to suit their individual requirements. Plain, stained and decorative glass is obtainable at craft shops, as is the self-adhesive copper strip which must be attached to each glass edge. Mastery of a wheeled cutter is quickly attained, but practice will be necessary for the effective use of a soldering iron. There is no framework, as such, for small terraria and the rigidity comes from the glass and the bond between the copper strip and a generous layer of solder. If an 'antique' rather than silver appearance is preferred, the solder can be easily treated with a suitable chemical. The advantages of making your own terrarium are a design to match your interior décor, the immense satisfaction of DIY, and the fact that it will have been a good deal less expensive than purchasing one.

Plant cases have an interesting history. In 1829 the London doctor, Nathaniel Ward, inadvertently discovered that a glass enclosure enabled the successful cultivation of plants which were otherwise difficult or even impossible to grow. He had put the chrysalis of a moth into a jar to study its metamorphosis. He also put soil in the jar before replacing the top. A fern subsequently appeared which flourished for some years, in marked contrast to similar plants which failed to

Fig 81   Terrarium, plants and materials.

survive the severe air pollution of the time. The fate of the moth is forgotten but the success of the fern gave rise to the increasing use of glass containers, particularly for transporting plants.

The heyday of plant collecting was the nineteenth century when specimens were gathered from all over the world for wealthy European clients. They were usually despatched by sailing ship, and you can imagine the plight of tropical plants lashed to the decks and subjected to all manner of climatic change during an eight-week voyage. Few survived to take root in foreign soil,

Fig 82 A terrarium with the top removed and showing the blue leaf of Strobilanthes, *an asparagus fern and ivy.*

but the subsequent use of so-called Wardian cases revolutionized the long-distance transportation of living plants. They escaped the Doldrums and rounded the Cape unscathed and without any special attention. While ornamental plants are the subject of this book it would be wrong not to pay homage to the part which the good doctor played in creating a British institution.

Wardian cases also made it possible for tea plants to be carried safely from China to India, thus allowing plantations to be established in various parts of the British Empire. One interesting footnote is that some years before Ward's accidental discovery, a Scotsman called Maconochie experimented with plants in a goldfish bowl and went on to construct a miniature greenhouse. To him goes the award for scientific endeavour, but Ward gets the glory because he publicized his findings in a book imaginatively entitled *On the Imitation of the Natural Conditions of Plants in Closely Glazed Cases*. The design of these utilitarian cases was copied and embellished by the Victorians, and they became a fashionable feature in the drawing rooms of the period. Wardian cases are still made, in modern form, but to see original examples you must visit museums. One excellent case is in the style of the Crystal Palace, and can be found in Glasgow's People's Palace museum. By the end of the nineteenth century the fashion declined and it is only recently that interest has been rekindled in custom-made display cases for plants. These are very beautiful but they are also very expensive.

The pleasure of having a plant sanctuary in the home is similar to that of owning a fish aquarium. Not only does it yield the fascination of watching interesting life forms in their own equable environment, it also provides a decorative centrepiece. Enthusiastic growers can heat and light the cases with the help of thermostats and time-switches, and the encapsulated plants can be given conditions which are virtually identical to their native habitat. It has often been said that an aquarium is a picture which is always changing;

Fig 83   Just another outdoor rock garden. . . ?

Fig 84   . . . Actually, it is part of a landscape which is enclosed in a very
large plant case belonging to the Reaseheath College of Agriculture, UK.

Fig 85   Everything you need for planting a fashionable terrarium – a
selection of plants, pot of compost, charcoal and gravel.

the same is true of a plant case or terrarium, but the change is more gradual. Initially it would be unwise to embark on the installation of a sophisticated plant case, but an inexpensive aquarium offers a realistic alternative which will be just as satisfactory for the plants. It is best to keep things simple to begin with, adding electrical devices later when knowledge and commitment have increased.

Unlike bottles and other enclosures with restricted access, a terrarium is easily planted and, perhaps more important, maintenance and subsequent changes are not a problem. Any plants which fail or later prove to be inappropriate can be removed and replaced. Whereas with bottles the planting must be

discarded in its entirety, the terrarium can be adjusted to meet new requirements.

Preparation

Cleaning is the initial task, largely to ensure that there are no pathogens taking advantage of the ideal conditions. Then a 2.5cm(1in) layer of washed gravel should cover the terrarium base, with charcoal chips on top. This is followed by the compost which need not be more than 5cm(2in) deep at the front, but two or three times deeper at the rear, depending on the height of the plants being grown. You will find that the effect is more interesting and natural if there is a rise in the 'ground' level from front to back.

Planting

Terraria, in contrast to bottles, give ample scope for imaginative plant displays and the use of fairly mature specimens. Larger plants will give an immediate effect of maturity and their use may be helpful for beginners because less consideration is required about the ultimate proportions of younger subjects.

So far I have been discussing conventional planting into compost, but there is a further option for owners of medium to large terraria. Small plants can remain in their pots which can be camouflaged by foliage or totally submerged in the compost. In time, these potted plants will root through the drainage holes into the surrounding compost, but they can be removed easily. Anyone who anticipates frequent changes in the display will find this a useful method of planting. Another consideration is deciding whether an encased landscape is envisaged; if so, a few well-placed rocks or pebbles will enhance the scene. Whether you want to include tiny bridges, pathways, miniature gazebos and a statuette of Buddha is, of course, up to you.

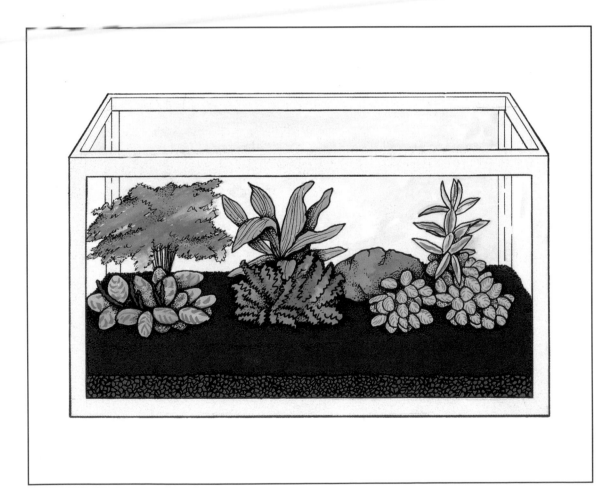

Fig 86 The depth of gravel and compost are shown here, together with the general principle of low plants being set at the front.

Fig 87   After planting with Fittonia, Ficus pumila, Dracaena sanderiana *and a small-leaved ivy.*

Fig 88   A terrarium planted with Hypoestes,
Ficus pumila *and ivy.*

Siting

As a terrarium is primarily ornamental it should
be placed for effect, but there will be limitations
imposed by the size of the structure. Some can
be suspended and others wall-mounted, but
generally the smaller decorative kinds can be
situated on shelves, tables or windowsills, always
bearing in mind the dangers of direct sunshine.
Converted aquaria are not so versatile in this
respect because they are usually larger, but the
one illustrated on page 00 is one of the smallest,
measuring just 45cm(18in) long by 25cm(10in)
deep, and 25cm(10in) high, and is therefore easily
moved. Larger examples and plant cases need
a more permanent site, and a decision must be
made whether there will be adequate natural
light throughout the year. If an area is too dark
then a large plant enclosure would not be a
viable proposition, unless artificial illumination is
provided. This problem is tackled at the end of
this chapter.

Maintenance

Even the smallest terrarium will have sufficient
access for hand pruning, and an aquarium will be
completely open at the top. Plant cases usually
have sliding glass doors at the front, and they can
easily be removed. This means that there are no
impediments to proper maintenance, and the
regular removal of debris, plant tidying and cleaning interior glass surfaces are accomplished with
ease. Watering will occasionally be necessary,
especially where a roofless structure is concerned, but otherwise is too rare to worry about.
And finally, note that in any long-standing display,
moss will probably invade. If you find it acceptable then no action is needed; in fact if desired,
it can be introduced at the outset. Other
gardeners will designate it a nuisance, in which
case it is quite easily removed at any time.

Artificial Lighting

The use of artificial light to grow plants, either as
the sole source or to supplement natural illumination, is prevalent in America but less popular in
other countries. The reason is not clear because
it is not a difficult business, and is a marvellous
way of supporting plant life in places which would
be otherwise completely hostile.

Supplementary Lights

In an open room many corners are too dark for
plants to thrive, but the use of spotlights will both
aid growth and enhance their appearance. While
light intensity might not be great it can certainly
supplement natural light and bridge the crucial
difference between meagre and healthy growth.

Incandescent bulbs (with tungsten filaments)
do not radiate that part of the light spectrum
which is ideal for plants, but they are better than
nothing. The biggest snag with ordinary bulbs is
that they give off considerable heat and therefore
cannot be placed too close to plants.

Fluorescent tubes, however, are desirable
because they combine high light output with low

Fig 89   This old fish tank becomes a terrarium, and is fitted with a canopy which houses the light fittings.

heat and are available in many shapes and sizes. They are most often used with shelving in such a way that the plant display is highlighted while the tubes are concealed from view. It is also possible to buy tastefully designed canopy fittings which can be suspended above a table or plant pedestal. Trolleys are also available, and give the novel possibility of illuminated plants on wheels.

Note that incandescent lighting and ordinary domestic fluorescent tubes are not ideal for plant growth. However, there is now a range of fittings which has been produced specifically for cultivating plants. Grow-Lux and Truelite tubes have been available for some years; Triton are more recent and new products are constantly coming

on the market. Many of these products have been designed for professional growers, while others have been targeted at the aquarium market, nonetheless being eminently suitable for domestic plants.

Mercury discharge lamps are another option and I believe that commercial plant growers use this high-intensity form of lighting more than any other, with at least a couple of manufacturers having the home grower in mind. These lamps are highly effective but are more obtrusive than fluorescent tubes and they do not blend easily with a domestic décor.

And finally I should emphasize that all the lighting systems which have been designed for

70

Fig 90   *This white-flowering example of* Lantana *does not change colour.*

growing plants can be used to supplement natural light, and can also be used as the sole source of illumination . . . which brings us to plant cases and large terraria.

Illuminated Enclosures

A display case or terrarium which is lit from an overhead canopy is an object of great beauty, and will attract constant admiration. It is quite feasible to achieve perfect results even where there is no natural light but it is imperative, in this case, to use those fittings which have been designed with plants in mind. These give out most of their light in the blue and red wavelengths which are required for the photosynthetic process, although the difference is hardly noticeable to the human eye.

Undoubtedly, the fluorescent tubes are most suited to plant cabinets and, as a rule, each 0.09sq m (1sq ft) of growing area will require about 15 watts of light output depending on the distance between the lights and plant level. If you want to be more scientific, use a photographic light meter and take a reading outdoors on a sunny day in a well-lit but shaded position. This will give you a good indication of what light level

is required at the base of the terrarium; otherwise, move your plant display to find the most suitable site. It will also be necessary to determine, by trial and error, what period of illumination is best suited to the plants you are growing, and a timeswitch will be essential when the proper duration of 'daytime' has been established.

All this may seem rather elaborate but there is no reason why the indoor gardener should not master these techniques in a very short time, particularly if the electricity industry's publications are consulted. Advice is also available from the manufacturers of lighting equipment, and the Houseplant Society will provide individual advice from experienced, amateur growers.

Cost is a potential deterrent to anyone contemplating the joys of illuminated indoor gardens because the prices of lighting equipment are not low, but once the initial purchase is made, the running costs are low. The lamps have an average life of about 9,000 hours, which probably means they will last for two years in normal use. A 125 watt lamp would give high light intensity over an area of 0.9sq m(10sq ft). Four, 76cm(30in) long tubes would be needed for the same output, and although the running costs might be slightly lower than the mercury lamp, the tubes have a life in excess of 7,500 hours.

It only remains to say that anyone considering an illuminated plant enclosure should also fit a heater; only a small one is needed, together with a thermostat, and the running costs would be negligible. Heat and artificial light will enable you to cultivate a portion of tropical terrain in even the darkest part of an unheated hall.

Do's and Don'ts

Do refer to the bottle garden list which is also applicable to terraria.
Do consider using artificial lighting in one way or another.
Do use terraria plants which have similar requirements.
Don't install electrical equipment unless you are competent to do so.

CHAPTER 4

Plants for Bottles, Terraria and Cases

The main consideration when choosing plants is obviously size and fortunately, depending on the constraints of the container, there is a good selection of suitable subjects. In every instance it is advisable to buy the smallest plants and face the inevitable day when they outgrow the available space. While dismantling may be the end of one display it allows the opportunity to prune or divide existing plants, or even make a completely fresh start. Each end is a new beginning.

Growing in glass enclosures is an excellent way of cultivating those subjects which will otherwise fail without adequate humidity, but some plants which were listed in Chapter 2 are sufficiently adaptable to fall into both categories and many will do even better in a protected environment. Perhaps I should repeat that flowering plants

Fig 91 When a green-tinted bottle is used, variegated and patterned foliage looks the most effective. Stromanthe *and* Fittonia *are seen here.*

Fig 92 Overhead view showing Asparagus plumosus *and* Selaginella, *with* Stromanthe amabilis *and* Fittonia argyroneura *'Nana'.*

should not be used where inaccessibility prevents the regular removal of spent blooms because of the ever-present threat of mould.

Acorus gramineus 'Pusillus' (sweet flag). Min 7.5°C(45°F). Bright/partial shade. The sweet flag described on page 17 is about 25cm(10in) tall, whereas this one is particularly useful for small containers, growing to about 5cm(2in).

Aglaonema (Chinese evergreen). Min 13°C (55°F). Partial shade. All the species have spear-shaped leaves but whilst *A. modestum* has plain foliage, most of the others have some variegation and the most popular is *A. crispum* 'Silver Queen'. All *Aglaonema* have the ability to survive in poor light, but they do become quite large so select a small, young plant.

Anthurium crystallinum (crystal anthurium). Min 16°C(60°F). Bright. The beautiful heart-shaped leaves with white veining can grow quite tall, and the plants can be temperamental but they do look magnificent in large cases.

Aphelandra squarrosa (zebra plant). Min 13°C (55°F). Bright. Although usually a windowsill subject, this is ideal for glass enclosures and the flowers last for a long time.

Begonia Min 13°C(55°F). Bright. All the flowering species are suited to humid containers (*see* Chapter 3) but there is also the opportunity to try the foliage varieties.

B. boweri (eyelash begonia) – has soft hairy, green leaves, and brown markings near the edges.
B. cleopatra – has almost palmate leaves which are predominantly brown with green marks.
B. masoniana (iron cross begonia) – a very distinctive and well-known species with a definite brown cross in the leaf centre.
B. rex – there are many Rex begonias in an incredible colour range and named varieties too, but only the small-leaved types should be chosen

Fig 93 *The most popular and versatile palm,* Neanthe bella, *with the striking foliage of a* Begonia rex.

because some are inclined to grow large in favourable conditions.

Bromeliads Min 10°C(50°F). Bright. All the bromeliads enjoy moist air and will be happy in glass containers, but perhaps *Cryptanthus acaulis* is the most versatile because of its compact habit.

Caladium Min 18.5°C(65°F). Bright. The sight of these plants is quite dazzling but it must be stressed that only large cabinets can house them – the leaves are often over 30cm(12in) long. The growth is from tubers, between spring and autumn, whereupon the foliage dies back for winter dormancy. The growing plants and even the tubers must always be above 16°C(60°F) and 6°C(10°F) warmer is probably the ideal.

73

Fig 94 *A magnificent* Caladium, *showing the varied colours and markings which occur on one plant. It is, however, a difficult subject to cultivate.*

Fig 95 Calathea *are difficult though spectacular plants. This large example of* C. 'Rosea Picta' *is showing signs of leaf damage, possibly due to an atmosphere which is too dry.*

Calathea Min 16°C(60°F). Partial shade. In my view these are the aristocrats amongst foliage plants, but they have proved very disappointing when grown in living-rooms. They must have constant warmth and humidity and must not be exposed to fluctuating temperatures or direct sunlight. In fact, they probably should not be attempted outside a terrarium or plant case where their magnificence can flourish. *C. mackoyana* (peacock plant) is commonly seen, albeit in distress! *C. ornata*, *C. insignis* and *C. zebrina* have similar, paper-thin leaves which are spectacularly patterned.

Chlorophytum comosum 'Variegatum' (spider plant). Min 7.5°C(45°F). Bright/partial shade. An excellent survivor in most circumstances, and will thrive in bottles and so on, but will soon outgrow the space.

Cissus discolour (begonia vine). Min 16°C (60°F). Partial shade. A delicate relative of the kangaroo vine which has exquisitely coloured leaves and is a strong contender for the starring role in any collection.

Codiaeum (croton). Min 10°C(60°F). Bright.

74

Fig 96 Calthea picturata.

Fig 97 Very similar to Calathea in its requirements, this Ctenanthe lubbersi has rather surrealist foliage. As far as I know it does not have a common name – how about the Picasso plant?

Outstanding leaf colour. There are many hybrids offered for sale, some with curious leaf shapes. The most common example is *C. variegatum* 'Pictum' which has reddish mature leaves, but eventually this plant will reach shrub proportions. Another good red colour is *C.* 'Reidii', whilst *C.* 'Bravo' and *C.* 'Craigii' have yellow variegations, the latter also with unusually shaped leaves.

Coffea (coffee plant). Min 10°C(50°F). Bright. An excellent subject with dark green, shiny leaves which are gently wrinkled. Note that it will outgrow limited space long before you can pick coffee beans, though pruning is simple and not resented.

Ctenanthe oppenheimiana 'Tricolour' (never, never plant). Min 16°C(60°F). Partial shade. A close relative of the *Maranta* and *Calathea* and equally demanding in its requirements for even warmth and humidity.

Cyperus (umbrella plant). Min 10°C(50°F).

Bright/partial shade. The most appealing feature of this plant is its shape which gives the appearance of a group of slender palms. It is grown in rooms where it must always be placed in a saucer containing water, but very often the leaf tips go brown because of low humidity. *C. alternifolius* can be 60cm(2ft) tall but the dwarf species, *C. diffusus*, can be accommodated in medium-size bottles and terraria.

Dieffenbachia (dumb cane). Min 16°C(60°F). Bright. *D. picta* 'Exotica' could also have been listed in the open-room category because it is quite tolerant of centrally-heated rooms, whereas others resent dry air, cold draughts, and fluctuating temperatures. Small plants in terraria look very handsome, but ultimately they will grow too

75

tall to be accommodated. Incidentally, the sap from these plants is poisonous and can cause strong allergic reactions if it comes into contact with skin.

Dizygotheca elegantissima (finger aralia). Min 10°C(60°F). Bright. True to name, this is an elegant foliage plant, if delicate. Although some households have successful examples in living-rooms, it appreciates the even conditions of cases and terraria.

Dracaena Min 13°C(55°F). Bright. A few Dracaena can manage in dry air (see Chapter 3), but most prefer warm humidity. However, names such as dragon tree and false palm indicate that a favourable regime will encourage rapid growth. Only one species is suited to confined spaces – D. sanderiana (ribbon plant) – its erect habit and white edged leaves make it an excellent contrast to creeping plants.

Episcia cupreata (flame violet). Min 16°C(60°F). Bright. Lovers of warmth and humidity, these plants are excellent for enclosed cultivation. They are dual purpose with interesting flowers and foliage. Another species, E. dianthiflora, has superb, dark green foliage and delicate white blooms which earn the name of lace flower. There are some highly desirable varities of Episcia, but sadly they are extremely difficult to obtain and to cultivate.

Exacum affine (Persian violet). Min 10°C(50°F). Bright. As described earlier, this is a neat, flowering plant which does not look out of place in bottles or other glass units. The foliage is agreeable and, if kept cool, will flower for weeks but as with all flowering subjects, the dead blooms must be picked off regularly.

Ferns Min 10°C(50°F). Bright/partial shade. Practically all ferns require a moist atmosphere and most will soon become miserable if they are cultivated in dry air. They are ideal for all kinds of glass containers and come in a wide range of size and form. There are hundreds of fern species which could be grown indoors, but relatively few are commercially available and the following selection embraces those most widely offered:

Adiantum – Maidenhairs are well known and frequently seen in hanging baskets. A. raddianum (delta maidenhair) has tiny leaflets and A. hispidulum (rose maidenhair) has conventional fronds which are pink whilst immature.
Asparagus – A. sprengeri, A. meyeri and A. plumosus are very common, and the latter is believed to be the most fern-like. Appearances, however, are deceptive because technically none of them is a true fern. Yet they serve the purpose well and tend to be more tolerant than real ferns.
Asplenium – A. nidus makes a glorious specimen but it is most unfern-like with long, arching leaves which have earned the title of bird's nest fern. There is a dwarf in this genus. A. fontanum (smooth rock spleenwort), which only grows 9cm(4in) tall, and A. bulbiferum (mother spleenwort) has the intriguing ability to grow miniature plants on its mature fronds.
Blechnum – B. gibbum grows like the head of a palm tree with stiff fronds, and as the plant ages a trunk develops too. A miniature form is B. penna-marina which has a creeping habit and is about 10cm(4in) high.
Ceterach – C. officinarum (scaly spleenwort) has thick fronds which are covered, on the underside, with brown scales.
Cyrtomium – C. falcatum has leaves which are holly-shaped and dark, glossy green. It looks marvellous when young but grows quite large and will have to leave the terrarium. Grows quite well in a cool room.
Davallia – D. canariensis (rabbit's foot fern) is a resilient fern whose common name derives from its creeping, rhizomatous roots.
Nephrolepsis – This genus includes the Boston fern, but most forms of N. exaltata are similar in looks.
Pellaea – P. rotundifola (button fern) has the perfect low-growing habit for bottles or small terraria.

Phyllitis – The species *P. scolopendrium* (hart's tongue fern) is a rather grand looking plant with long, smooth leaves which have wavy edges.

Polystichum – *P. acrostichioides* (Christmas fern) is an upright grower with pointed fronds.

Pteris – One of the most charming and easily grown ferns is *P. cretica* (ribbon fern), and two other forms *P. cretica* 'Albolineata' and *P. cretica* 'Cristata' are similarly simple to grow. *P. ensiformis* 'Victoriae' (silver lace fern) is a lovely plant with white centres to the leaflets.

The enormous variety of shape and texture in ferns means that it is entirely possible to create a superb display even if no other type of plant is used. Conversely, whatever the subjects in a collection, a fern can be found to complement them.

Ficus   Min 13°C(55°F). Partial shade. Most of the ornamental fig family, which includes the rubber plants, have aspirations to become trees or major shrubs and most grow happily as houseplants, but some appreciate moist air and are diminutive. *F. pumila* (creeping fig) is superb for bottles and all other enclosures, and the variegated form is especially desirable. *F. radicans* 'Variegata' trails and has larger leaves, but is just as suitable.

Fittonia   Min 13°C(55°F). Partial shade. Creeping, compact growth and leaves with contrasting veins are the main characteristics. There are two species, *F. verschaffeltii* (painted net leaf) which is the more colourful and *F. argyroneura*, (silver net leaf) which is very attractive. There is also a dwarf

Fig 98   Young seedlings from a strain of Hypoestes *which is appropriately called 'Pink Splash'. These plants are easily grown from seed.*

form of the latter called the snakeskin plant which is reasonably well fitted for open-room life, but it is also very successful in bottles and terraria.

Gynura (velvet plant). Min 10°C(50°F). Bright. Although a natural climber, *G. sarmentosa* is usually grown where it can creep amongst other subjects and show off its attractive foliage. The leaves are red-green and are covered in purple hairs so that the overall effect changes slightly when the light strikes from different directions. The plant does have a serious drawback – the small orange flowers smell really awful and it is sensible to remove them before they open.

Hedera (ivy). Min 4.5°C(40°F). Bright/partial shade. The ivies deserve their reputation as tenacious houseplants, but they do not relish centrally-heated dryness and their performance is greatly enhanced by more sympathetic treatment. Those with small leaves are most suitable for enclosed cultivation.

Helxine soleirolii (mind your own business). Min 7.5°C(45°F). Bright/partial shade. This is often grown as a carpet plant in terraria, but each plant should carry a warning: other plants will be overpowered unless *Helxine*'s territorial ambitions are occasionally curbed by cutting back. Having said that, it is a most adaptable patch of greenery, decidedly unfussy about light levels and temperature.

Hypoestes sanguinolenta (polka-dot plant). Min 13°C(55°F). Bright. One of the most regular inhabitants of bottle gardens and terraria because of its happy disposition and pink-spotted foliage, but the strength of colouring is dependent upon bright light. In poor light the green is more evident than the pink, but it is still a welcome sight and the tendency to grow rather shapelessly is easily modified by pinching out the growing tips. There are a number of seed strains now available which produce extremely pink plants; their germination and culture is not difficult.

Fig 99 *The most commonly grown* Maranta *is* M. kerchoveana, *known as rabbit tracks. It is also called the prayer plant because the leaves tend to fold together at night time.*

Iresine herbstii (blood leaf). Min 13°C(55°F). Bright. The blood-red leaves are quite startling, but again the colour is dependent on bright conditions and preferably sunshine. Of course it would be unwise to position a bottle or terrarium in sunshine because the interior temperature would soar to plant-killing heights; maximum light without sun is the best which can be achieved. Even in a good situation *Iresine* tends to become leggy but a temporary display is worth the effort. There is another species, *I. herbstii aureoreticulata*, which is less demanding but the leaves are yellow and green.

Kalanchoe blossfeldiana (flaming Katy). Min 10°C(50°F). Bright. Previously listed in another category, this is one of few flowering plants which can be recommended for growing behind glass. The flowering period is long and the foliage is

Fig 100   *The olive-green leaves of* Maranta tricolour *gradually turn a darker shade, but the red herringbone markings remain vivid.*

Fig 101   *The neat symmetry of* Mimosa *leaves which fold up when touched.*

attractive – when the plant grows too large it can be removed and potted up as a houseplant.

Maranta   Min 10°C(50°F). Partial shade. Two kinds are commonly grown – *M. leuconeura kerchoveana* which is either called rabbit tracks or prayer plant, and *M. leuconeura erythrophylla* (herringbone plant). The former has pairs of brown blotches on the leaves and the latter has red veins. Less well known is *M. leuconeura massangeana* which has very dark green leaves and silvery-white veining. All dislike sunshine and cold and dry air, and although they are frequently grown as houseplants, leaf damage is usually evident and indicates the desire for more equable surroundings.

Mimosa pudica (sensitive plant). Min 13°C (55°F). Bright. This species was brought to

Fig 102 Unlike most others in the Peperomia *family,* P. magnoliaefolia *is succulent-like, with fleshy and glossy variegated leaves.*

Europe from Barbados in 1638 by the younger John Tradescant, and has fascinated the world's gardeners ever since because its leaves fold when touched. The feathery leaflets are most elegant but the plant has a rather bare look, especially as it matures.

Nertera depressa (bead plant). Min 4.5°C (40°F). Bright. It looks a little like *Helxine* with the bonus of tiny orange berries in autumn and winter. Plants are often expensive but, with care, they will live for a few years.

Palms Min 10°C(50°F). Bright/partial shade. *Neanthe bella* has already been listed as an open-room plant, but it is also the most suitable palm for growing in glass units. A possible alternative is *Cocos weddelliana*, (dwarf coconut palm), which takes about 20 years to reach its ultimate height of 18m(6ft) or so, and is graceful at all stages of its growth.

Pellionia Min 13°C(55°F). Bright/partial shade. These plants come from the forest floors of Burma and Vietnam. Two species have colourful foliage, *P. pulchra* with brown veining and *P. daveauna* with brown edging to the leaves. The latter has the misleading common name of watermelon begonia.

Peperomia Min 10°C(50°F). Bright/partial shade. Slow-growing, compact and comparatively easy to care for, this group of plants is ideal for enclosed cultivation but most of the species are susceptible to excessive watering. *P. caperata* (emerald ripple) is aptly named, and there is also a variegated form. Other bushy types are *P. hederaefolia* (ivy peperomia) and *P. argyreia* which is either called watermelon peperomia or, more imaginatively, the rugby football plant. Unlike the above species are *P. magnoliaefolia* (desert privet) and *P. obtusifolia* (baby rubber plant), which are both succulent in appearance; so too is the trailing species *P. rotundifolia*. Two other creeping or trailing kinds are *P. prostrata* and *P. scandens*.

Pilea Min 10°C(50°F). Bright/partial shade. *P. cadierei* (aluminium plant) is the most illustrious member of this family, but there are others also excellent for bottles and terraria – *P. involucrata* (friendship plant or panamiga) and *P. repens* (black leaf panamiga). Other similar species with highly decorative, crinkled leaves are *P. mollis* (moon valley) and *P.* 'Bronze' with its lovely brown and green leaves, and silver centres. All these plants grow less attractive with age but they are easily propagated from cuttings, and this is true of two different *Pilea*, *P. depressa* (creeping Jenny) and *P. nummularia*, (creeping Charlie) which both have small leaves and a creeping or trailing habit.

Piper ornatum Min 16°C(60°F). Partial shade. Has exquisite foliage, green with pink and silver markings, and is a climbing ornamental pepper though is often difficult to grow.

Fig 103 Polyscias are commercially propagated from cane cuttings giving them a 'tree-like' appearance from an early age. This variegated version is P. balfouriana.

Plectranthus oertendahlii (Swedish ivy). Min 10°C(50°F). Partial shade/shade. This species has been mentioned for its versatility and it may become rather rampant in a protected environment. Pruning is simple and will prevent it from abusing your hospitality.

Pleomele Min 13°C(55°F). Bright/partial shade. To avoid any problems with the classification of this genus, it is included here and under the more accurate name of *Dracaena*. *P. reflexa* (song of India) has been described but two others may be encountered: *P. thalioides* with plain green, spear-shaped leaves, and *P. angustifolia honorariae* whose leaves are more slender and are almost brown with light coloured margins.

Polyscias Min 13°C(55°F). Bright. Very handsome tropical trees which grow sufficiently slowly for our purposes and look like examples of bonsai because they are most often grown on woody stems. *P. fruiticosa* (Ming aralia), has fern-like leaves whilst the more popular *P. balfouriana* (dinner plate aralia) has rounded, variegated leaves.

Rhoeo discolor (boat lily). Min 10°C(50°F). Bright/partial shade. Long, glossy, lanceolate leaves with purple undersides; occasional flowers at the base of the plant which are more or less boat-shaped. As a young specimen it will fit in well with any collection but eventually the leaves reach 30cm (1ft).

Saintpaulia (African violet). Min 13°C(55°F). Bright. A hugely popular houseplant and probably the most common flowering subject for bottles and terraria. Enclosed conditions suit them, and particularly where artificial light is permanently available plants will be in bloom almost the whole year. Specialist nurseries offer a huge range of varieties including some which are truly miniature, less than 7.5cm(3in) across.

Sansevieria hahnii (bird's nest sanseveiria). Min 10°C(50°F). Bright/partial shade. The large

species are clearly unsuited to restricted spaces, but *S. hahnii* has compact rosettes with interesting foliage and the variegated version has a bright appearance.

Saxifraga sarmentosa (mother of thousands). Min 4.5°C(40°F). Bright. This species has green leaves with white veins, but the 'Tricolour' form is much more attractive with its red edges, though somewhat more tender. Both produce 'thousands' of young plants at the ends of runners, and both are pendulous by nature but will

Fig 104 Syngonium is usually grown as a bushy houseplant, but it is a climber and forms a tower of foliage with the help of a mosspole. This variety is 'Silver Knight'.

be happy to creep over the compost instead.

Selaginella martensii (creeping moss). Min 13°C(55°F). Partial shade. Another regular member of bottle garden communities which has been a favourite since Victorian times. It can be found in various golden and green forms. Each plant develops into a neat, low hummock of vegetation but is somewhat invasive. There is a different species, S. uncinata (peacock fern) whose foliage is perhaps more fern-like than moss-like.

Siderasis fuscata (brown spiderwort). Min 13°C(55°F). Bright. Often grouped with Tradescantia, this plant has green leaves which are covered in brown hairs and stripes, tinged with red. It is a rosette-forming plant which will not exceed its allotted space.

Smithiana hybrida (temple bells). Min 16°C (60°F). Bright. Although success is possible in an open room, this performs much better in the confines of a warm terrarium. When the plants have died down, the rhizomes should be removed and stored dry and cool for a couple of months before replanting.

Streptocarpus saxorum (false African violet). Min 10°C(55°F). Bright. This is unlike the usual Streptocarpus and has a mass of succulent leaves and occasional flowers which are typical of the genus. The plant may be difficult to obtain but is easily propagated from leaf cuttings.

Strobilanthes (Persian shield). Min 13°C(55°F). Bright. This plant has only made an appearance recently and there is every likelihood that it will become extremely popular, especially as a colourful foliage subject for bottles and terraria.

The leaves are olive green with quite regular, mauve markings between the veins, and the plants have a usefully bushy shape. Away from direct sunshine and very low humidity the plants tolerate an open room, but growth is reluctant and the leaves remain small. In glass enclosures the plants luxuriate with larger leaves and more intense colouring.

Syngonium podophyllum (goosefoot plant). Min 13°C(55°F). Bright/partial shade. A relative of the Philodendron, Syngonium is a climber and although it is grown with partial success as a normal houseplant, it does not revel in dry air. Young plants look well in plant cases because the leaf markings are at their most prominent; this quality diminishes with age as does the characteristic goosefoot leaf shape which changes to palmate form. Named varieties which have superb variegations are: 'Silver Knight', 'Imperial White' and 'Green Gold', but there is also one with green leaves called 'Emerald Green'.

Tolmiea menziesii (piggy-back plant). Min 4.5°C(40°F). Bright/partial shade. This has been listed earlier as a plant with great survival characteristics and it will serve admirably in terraria (with the proviso that steps are taken to limit the inevitable expansion which results from ideal conditions).

Tradescantia (wandering jew). Min 7.5°C (45°F). Bright. Most of the Tradescantia are undemanding plants and will prosper in a variety of conditions, but they should not be forgotten as candidates for bottles and terraria. Growth may be vigorous in warm and moist surroundings but growing tips are easily removed to stop the plants from wandering too far.

CHAPTER 5

Orchids in the Home

The reputations of many plants have suffered over the years from myths and disinformation, but the greatest damage has been done to orchids. They are undoubtedly the most glamorous members of the plant kingdom but they have been closely associated, in the minds of most people, with wealth and specialized cultivation. Historically these associations are accurate, and there was a time when the rich were seduced by the exotic splendour of orchid blooms and paid huge sums of money for imported specimens from the Far East. Since then costs have reduced considerably. Not only that, most of the orchids on sale are grown in the country of purchase and more efficient propagation has meant that their real cost is lower than ever before. Nonetheless, the old image prevails and the twin deterrents of expense and difficulty have prevented a proper recognition of orchids as plants for everyone.

There are probably in excess of 100,000 species and hybrids in cultivation, but although most of them do originate in tropical climates it is wrong to assume that they all need the highest temperatures and humidity as well as a high degree of growing skill. Very many popular orchids will flourish in minimum night temperatures between 10–16°C(50–60°F) and a daytime range of 18–30°C(65–85°F), a level of warmth commonplace in many living-rooms. Humidity is certainly important and by using a gravel tray and keeping plants in close proximity you will succeed. Many enthusiasts do use growing cases for showing and growing their collections, but good results are possible without such refinements.

It cannot be denied that in comparison with the majority of houseplants, orchids are more costly but their value for money is very high indeed. A flowering-size plant may be three times more expensive than, for example, a cyclamen, but consider the additional benefits. The lifespan of orchid blooms is legendary, and many varieties produce numerous flowers which last 8–10 weeks. Some will flower twice annually, and with careful maintenance the plants will live for many years. Propagation too is practicable from orchids of some genera.

Although newcomers to orchid culture may be tempted by the lower prices of seedlings and young plants, I am sure the best plan is to purchase those which are flowering or just about to do so. Mature plants are easier to cultivate and the excitement of a prolonged display of flowers will stimulate the new grower to learn the likes and dislikes of the orchid family. With this experience you can progress to younger plants which may need a few years of cultivation before they reach flowering size.

I would recommend that, initially at least, plants are bought from specialist nurseries which will guarantee the quality of their stock, and will be able to give advice — before and after purchase. Some of the growers may specialize in particular kinds of orchid, but all have a representative selection and it is likely that first-time buyers will be able to choose from the following genera.

Cymbidium These are the most popular orchids throughout the world, and the long sprays of flowers are used as a corsage or as cut blooms. The common name of boat orchids derives from the shape of the lip or lower petal, and not because of their origins, which is mainly the

Fig 105 An orchid display staged for a local orchid society.

Fig 106 A spectacularly marked Miltonia, 'Gascoigne' × 'Cindy Kane'.

Fig 107 An impressive arrangement of orchids, mainly including Phalaenopsis and Miltonia, with some Odontoglossum.

Indian Himalayas. A bright room with some sunshine suits *Cymbidium*, and a winter minimum temperature of 10°C(50°F) is satisfactory, although extra warmth is beneficial as the plants come into flower. Broadly, two types are recognized — the standards which have long flower spikes and develop into big plants, and the miniatures which are more suitable for home culture.

Miltonia They come from Brazil and Colombia and are popularly called pansy orchids. They have rounded and flattened flowers and, in most cases, the stature of the plants means that they are suitable for medium-size terraria. A minimum temperature of 13°C(55°F) will keep these orchids happy.

86

Odontoglossum Most species come from high altitudes of tropical South and Central America, and sometimes attract the name of princess of the Andes. The modern hybrids which have been bred are excellent for beginners because they tolerate varying temperatures, but they do prefer it to be warmer than the mountains of their ancestors.

Paphiopedilum These are ladies' slipper orchids and come from south-east Asia. Before the majority were reclassified they were called *Cypripedium*, a name still widely used. The distinctive feature of the flowers is a modified lower petal which is pouch-shaped, and many varieties have slightly striped or mottled foliage. Of the orchid genera mentioned here, *Paphiopedilum* can be grown in lower light levels, but again a minimum temperature of 13°C(55°F) is needed.

Phalaenopsis The so-called moth orchids are also native to south-east Asia. Their hybrids are often recommended to new orchid growers because of the compact habit, tolerance and regular flowering ability. Like the *Odontoglossum*, 13°C(55°F) is a sensible minimum, but they can stand colder temperatures for short periods.

There are many other orchids which are suitable for growing in the home, apart from the five genera listed above, but to name them would make decisions complicated. No species or varieties have been mentioned for the same reason. Many nurseries breed orchids and therefore there is a tendency to specialize in certain genera and to produce particular, named varieties. The best course of action is to see the plants flowering, fall in love with one or more,

Fig 108 A display, mostly of Odontoglossum.

and then ask whether it would be suited to life in your lounge. In which case it would be helpful to know something of the basic culture and general requirements of orchids. Enthusiasts put a high priority on a greenhouse for maintaining plants in peak condition, however, orchids are more capable of coping with the home environment than many other subjects.

ORCHID CARE

Temperature

The temperatures associated with the recommended genera are preferred minima, but occasional variations below those figures will not matter, especially if the compost is kept fairly dry. The ideal orchids for home cultivation are those which are described as cool or intermediate types, but a windowsill in winter, particularly behind curtains, can become uncomfortably cold. Draughts are harmful as are heat sources such as radiators and fires, so the plants should not be close enough to suffer large fluctuations of temperature. Anything higher than about 30°C(85°F) is undesirable, and protection is necessary against scorching summer sunshine.

Light

The majority of orchids require some direct sunlight and a bright situation which is best achieved by using a south-facing windowsill during the winter, and an east or west aspect in the summer. If a south-facing position is unavoidable from May to September, then some shading will be necessary otherwise the plants will be better in a partially shaded spot outdoors. It is possible to maintain orchids in good health without sunshine but their flowering ability will suffer.

Humidity

This is a vital ingredient for success with most plants, and orchids are no exception. They will benefit from being grouped with other plants in your collection, but the surest way of providing moist air is to use a gravel tray which is merely a shallow container with gravel or small stones. The gravel should be kept permanently wet but there must be no water at the base of the plant pot otherwise capillary action will make the compost waterlogged. This problem is overcome either by ensuring that the water level is always below the top of the gravel or by placing the pot on a small saucer.

Water

As usual this is a troublesome factor, and it is impossible to give precise information about the regularity of watering. Many orchids are epiphytic, living with their roots wrapped around tree branches and not in soil, and although there is abundant natural rainfall the roots are only wet whilst rain is falling. Cultivated orchids are grown in specially formulated compost which is very coarse and quick-draining, but nevertheless it is essential to ensure that it is not permanently wet. Ideally, watering should be thorough, allowing surplus moisture to drain away. The compost should be allowed to become almost dry before repeating the process. The golden rule is, if in doubt leave well alone; a period of dryness at the roots is far preferable to soggy compost. Most orchid growers believe that rainwater is desirable and also that the water should be at room temperature to avoid chilling the roots of the plants.

Feeding

Orchid nurseries feed their plants regularly but this is another potential pitfall for the amateur grower – liquid feeds must always be used at half their normal dilution. If this is applied at every other watering *only during times of active growth*, the results are beneficial. Do remember though that over-feeding is seriously damaging to any plant.

Repotting

This will probably be necessary every year and should be carried out in the spring, using specially prepared orchid compost. This is better purchased from specialists until you feel sufficiently experienced to make up your own, but it is no longer an expensive item. At one time, osmunda fibre was imported from Japan for the purpose, but nowadays fir bark, coarse peat and polystyrene are used.

The old compost should be removed from the roots, and the opportunity taken to cut off any which are dead. A slightly larger pot is then selected which will hold the roots easily, but without giving undue space; the plants will do much better if the root run is slightly restricted rather than having too much room.

Propagation

The majority of orchids have what is called a sympodial habit of growth. This means that they regenerate from the base of old growths which usually takes the form of pseudobulbs. A mature plant will have many of these modified bulbs, and some of the older ones can be cut away during the repotting procedure and used for propagation. Typically, the severed bulbs are placed in a plastic bag together with moist sphagnum moss and placed somewhere which is consistently warm. When new growth is evident the bulb can be potted up using an orchid compost mix. Other orchids have a growth pattern described as monopodial which means a single growth appears from a rhizome. In many cases propagation is difficult, but sometimes the upper part of the plant will form roots and these can then form the basis of a new plant.

Pests

In comparison with other plants, orchids are relatively pest-free, but it is as well to be prepared for any attacks which might take place. Aphids are certainly possible visitors and whitefly

Fig 109 *This orchid case contains* Paphiopedilums *at the front, with a cluster of* Phalaenopsis *flowers behind.*

are not unknown, but scale insect is probably the most insistent pest and, unless detected, can reach damaging proportions. Earwigs should also be mentioned although they are not, fortunately, prevalent indoors. Insecticide sprays when necessary will control all but the adult scale insects – these can only really be controlled using a small sponge and methylated spirits.

A Case for Orchids

The cultivation of orchids in an open room can be entirely successful if basic principles are observed, although they are also eminently suited to displaying in growing cases. Unlike

Fig 110 An orchid case, with a sliding front, removable panel and a fibreglass 'rock face' at the rear with recesses to hold plants.

aquaria, which will perhaps need to be incorporated in an aesthetically pleasing arrangement, growing cases can stand alone as impressive pieces of furniture and be the focal point of the interior décor. The framework is invariably high-quality hardwood and provision is made for ventilation and lighting in the top of the cabinet. Despite being expensive they will last a lifetime, and for enthusiastic cultivators it can be an investment which will return decades of enjoyment and attract widespread admiration.

Phalaenopsis, *Miltonia* and *Paphiopedilum* are the favourite orchids for growing cases on account of their modest stature. However, I have seen a number of cases which are over 90cm(3ft) tall, and so there are no limits to the genera

which can be accommodated. As permanent occupants of terraria and cabinets, orchids will not flower satisfactorily unless there is supplementary lighting, though they can be grown elsewhere and displayed when in bloom. To cultivate them over the long term in cases will require some experimentation so that the intensity and duration of the lighting can be determined. Growing healthy plants in controlled conditions is not difficult, but to achieve a regular flowering display you will need a degree of experience.

Electrical elements wired to a thermostat make heating completely automatic but you must also consider ventilation and humidity. This can take the form of a reservoir containing stones and water which is positioned above the heat source, and the required exchange of air is either by adjustable louvres or an electric fan. The net result is a contained tropical climate with adjustable temperature, variable humidity and a daylength which is controlled by a timeswitch.

The decorative variations are infinite, involving the introduction of other plants, with similar climatic requirements, to act as an integrated backcloth for the exotic colours of the orchid blooms. The back wall of the cabinet allows the use of a rock face, usually made of fibreglass, which gives an authentic look to the display. These background units can have nooks and crevices, at various heights, into which mosses or trailing subjects can be planted, or they can accommodate those orchids which prefer to be closer to the light source. Purists can also use growing cases with sections of tree branches so that epiphytic plants can be grown in the way that nature intended; in short, you can have a piece of jungle in the lounge.

For a beginner these somewhat high-tech features may seem rather daunting, but they are very exciting and can lead to an all-consuming hobby. Indeed, I offer the warning that controlled environment cultivation can be addictive. The potential difficulties of growing cases, artificial light and orchids have all been encountered before and newcomers can find ample advice

Fig III Pleione formosana *is a hardy orchid which is admirable for pot work and forms a useful clump within a couple of years.*

and encouragement from members of a local orchid society.

ORCHID FOOTNOTE

Orchids in the genus *Pleione* are widely available and since they originate in the Himalayas and parts of south-east Asia, will tolerate low temperatures. They will grow well on cold windowsills and, if the compost is not wet, will accept near freezing temperatures. Spring is the normal flowering time and the blooms are exquisite, although they do not last as long as those of tropical orchids. In a cool position the flowers will last for two to three weeks.

CHAPTER 6

African Violets

Of the 200 or so plants which are mentioned in this book, none deserves special attention more than *Saintpaulia ionantha*, the African violet. There is ample evidence to support the belief that this is the most popular houseplant in the world and its many virtues justify this position. There are societies in many countries of the world which are devoted to the cultivation of this plant — in Australia, Canada, the United States and the United Kingdom. Some of these organizations include the word gesneriad in their titles, signifying that *Saintpaulia* is the foremost member of the Gesneriaceae family which includes other illustrious and important houseplants such as *Achimenes*, *Collumnea*, *Episcia*, *Hypocyrta*, *Sinningia*, *Smithiana* and *Streptocarpus*. All have exquisite flowers and attractive foliage and although it could be argued that others have more spectacular blooms, it is undeniable that African violets are the most versatile, robust and tolerant gesneriads.

The plants were discovered in the mountains of East Africa 100 years ago in 1892 and were named after the German who found them — Baron Walter von Saint-Illaire. However, it was not until the 1920s that their potential as houseplants was realized and the initial impression of a neat, compact and long-flowering subject has been sustained and even improved. These characteristics convey accurately the versatility of African violets as plants which occupy little space, are conveniently housed in a wide range of glass enclosures and have the ability to flower throughout the year.

Blue, in all its shades, is the principal colour of the flowers but there are also pinks, reds, whites and bicolours. There are different types of bloom, from singles and doubles to those with crested centres or with frilly edges to the petals. Some variation in the foliage exists, with light or dark green leaves and more recently, new varieties have been bred which have notable variegations. The leaves have significant appeal being almost round or heart-shaped and they have a velvety texture which is produced by minute hairs on the upper surface. In some varieties, the underside is a deep maroon colour. The plants which are mass produced for general houseplant sales are of a very high standard, but for the enthusiast who is prepared to consult a specialist catalogue there is an intriguing selection on offer. Over the last decades, hundreds of named varieties have been bred and the process continues with new ones emerging every year.

As well as producing new varieties of *Saintpaulia*, the plant breeders have also been able to improve their constitution so that modern strains are much more robust and better able to resist the pressures of domesticity.

GROWING CONDITIONS

Gesneriads need warmth, humidity and shade from strong light but the new generations of *Saintpaulia* certainly can tolerate a regime which is less moist and includes some sunshine. Good light is essential and sunshine is beneficial as long as it is not relentless; however, the foliage must be dry otherwise it will scorch. More importantly, saintpaulias are responsive to artificial light which is why they will often flower during the winter even without special lighting. Adequate warmth is imperative and unless a minimum of

65°F (17°C) is maintained, the plant's flowering potential will not be realized. However, if the compost is kept reasonably dry there is no question that saintpaulias can survive cold conditions albeit with a dejected and lacklustre appearance. They can thrive in an open room situation especially on a gravel tray and in a suitable position, but the plants will look better and flower more prolifically in the confines of a bottle or terrarium.

PROPAGATION

Propagation is fairly simple using a variety of methods and the vegetative techniques are outlined in Chapter 8, but new plants are readily raised from seed. Most of the major seed companies offer at least one strain out of about two dozen which are currently available. Older strains are regularly replaced by new ones and nowadays, hybrids with variegated foliage and those with the various types of flowers can be obtained. Particularly notable are the miniatures which make fascinating pot subjects and will not outgrow a 2½in(6cm) container. These are magnificent additions to a small bottle garden collection.

The seed is very tiny and care is needed for a thin sowing which should be only over the surface of the compost. Very light watering is required and is best achieved by using a fine spray so that the seed is settled into place without being submerged in the compost. If the container is then placed in a plastic bag, the humid atmosphere will ensure that the compost does not dry out. If a temperature between 65–70°F (17–21°C) is maintained, germination should take place in 3–5 weeks.

A late-winter or early-spring sowing is ideal because the resultant plants will begin to flower in about six months and if agreeable conditions are provided, blooms should continue through the first winter. Seedlings grow slowly but reliably and when they can be handled easily, they should be potted individually using a peat-based compost. African violets have quite shallow roots and it is better if they are planted in the so-called half-pots; 3½–4in(10cm) pots will be needed for mature plants of the normal varieties and 2–2½in (6cm) pots for the miniatures. Frequent potting on is not desirable because although the plants will perhaps thrive, vigorous growth usually inhibits flower production. When the pot is well filled with roots, almost all potted plants will flower more abundantly and this is certainly true of African violets.

Seed-raised plants are an excellent alternative to the 'ordinary' strains which are sold by garden centres but if a passion develops for the plants along with a desire to grow the choice and unusual varieties, then contact will have to be made with specialist nurseries. The houseplant and saintpaulia societies, in various countries, usually have lists of the hybrids currently in cultivation and where they can be obtained.

CHAPTER 7

Practical Plant Care

The general needs of plants have been discussed earlier, but obviously it is when theory is put into practice that mistakes are made and problems arise. Some adverse factors take their toll quite quickly, and others bring about a gradual deterioration in plants. Regular inspection is paramount to spot the first signs of pests, diseases and the results of poor cultivation.

MAINTENANCE

Hygiene

Keeping plants neat and tidy is excellent practice for not only does it preserve their appearance, it is also instrumental in maintaining good health. No matter how expert your care may be, leaves will turn yellow and die; with some subjects this happens relatively quickly while with others it may take years. This occurrence is inevitable, irreversible and totally natural, and is not necessarily due to inferior treatment. The lowest leaves die first and should be removed promptly, though they often drop without assistance. If you are sure that the plant is healthy there is no cause for concern, but remember that over-watering will also lead to leaf shedding and so too will excessive dryness. Long-lived foliage as found on a *Monstera* and rubber plant will get dusty and should be cleaned periodically. Plants that have tough, shiny leaves should be wiped with a sponge and tepid water, or a proprietary liquid can be used. Other subjects have profiled or hairy leaves which can be maintained with a soft, dry bush, or the plant can stand outside to benefit from a summer shower.

Pruning

For many gardeners this horticultural branch of surgery gives rise to feelings of apprehension, but it should be viewed as a technique for improvement and sometimes as a life saver. You may be removing inferior growth after the winter or reducing the size of vigorous specimens, but whatever the reason pruning is an invigorating and rejuvenating process. It can be used to promote a desirable growth pattern in an otherwise unruly subject, and it should be appreciated that if a leading shoot is removed growth will appear lower down and the result will be bushiness rather that elongation. Secateurs can be used for woody stems but a sharp knife or razor blade must be used for soft growth, otherwise undue damage will result.

Repotting

For those plants which are grown in pots there comes the time when repotting becomes desirable or even essential. For vigorous subjects it might be an annual event, but remember that moving to a larger pot will encourage further growth. If you want to curtail the expansion or at least reduce it, repotting can be delayed but bear in mind that restricted root space will increase the requirements of water and nutrients. An alternative is called top dressing and entails the careful removal of the top inch or so of the old compost, replacing it with new soil. Using the existing pot in this process denies the opportunity for rapid root development but replenishes reserves of nutrients. The peat-based composts are the most commonly available and

Fig 112 Desirable equipment: (a) a maximum/minimum thermometer and a normal one; (b) a moisture meter; and (c) a narrow spout watering can.

wholly suitable for most plants, but it is vital not to compress this material unduly. Its effectiveness depends on its natural structure, and if it is compacted, aeration of the root area is reduced and waterlogging is possible. Spring is usually the best time for potting-on when the plant is beginning to be active, but it can be undertaken at any time whilst growth is underway. It is advisable not to repot when plants are dormant because the extra compost will be unused until the roots spread, and it may therefore be wet or stagnant.

For bottle gardens and terraria renewing the compost is impractical and undesirable because it would quickly encourage plants to outgrow their space. When these enclosed gardens are overgrown or the plants have deteriorated, they should be emptied and completely replanted.

Watering

Plants which are enclosed (or almost so) by glass may need watering occasionally, but it is vital that only a small amount is added as any excess is impossible to remove quickly. Using a small hand sprayer is the safest way to water bottle gardens, terraria and growing cases.

95

In the summer, open-room plants will need watering frequently and it is true that active growth and higher rates of evaporation will make over-watering unlikely, but it remains the major cause of plant failure in the home. The best advice to follow is to avoid watering routinely, and only do so when observation indicates it is necessary. Invariably the surface compost dries out long before the moisture is depleted within the rootball, and a cursory glance around the base of the plant will be misleading. Tabs are available which can be inserted into the compost, and they change colour as the degree of moisture varies. They are helpful indicators but for greater precision you may want to invest in a moisture meter. This is a long-lasting device with a probe which is inserted into the compost and which gives a reading on a dial; it is significant how this reading varies according to the depth of the probe.

Irrespective of whether you use a watering aid, the important rule is: do not water at fixed intervals. If there is any doubt about requirements, do not water because the effects of dryness are, for most subjects, slight and temporary. When you do water, do it thoroughly. In winter when there is a real danger of waterlogging, do not be nervous about allowing plants to be virtually dry for most of the time.

Feeding

In the context of plant life the term feeding is somewhat misleading because food is manufactured in the cells using hydrogen and carbon dioxide as the raw materials, light as the energy source and chlorophyll as the agent. What gardeners refer to as nutrients are perhaps better identified as those chemicals which aid natural processes and support healthy growth (call them vitamin supplements or tonics if you wish!). There are many trace elements which are necessary, and initially they are present in the compost but watering leaches them away and they are depleted as the plant grows. The minerals must be replenished but gardeners should beware the danger of constantly feeding plants. The outcome can be a rooting medium which is saturated with various chemicals and becomes toxic to plant life. What happens is that the concentrated solution around the roots causes sap to leave the plant leading to dehydration and fairly rapid death.

Liquid fertilizer is most often used but its convenience does seem to encourage over-application by over-attentive cultivators. If you can discipline yourself to apply a properly dilute solution every couple of weeks — but only during the growing season — all will be well. Otherwise it is preferable to use the pellets or sticks which are pushed into the compost and release small amounts of nutrient whenever the plant is watered.

Plant Positioning

If the advice is followed of buying a plant for a particular position in the home the main problems of light and temperature will be countered. However, if the plant ails it can be extremely difficult to identify the precise cause and only a process of elimination can help.

Pale leaves and weak growth indicate poor light and/or excessive warmth, and these factors must be considered separately. Moving the plant is a priority and if you believe that the malaise is due to incorrect light, reposition it in a brighter spot which is at about the same temperature as before. Watch carefully for a couple of weeks to see if there is an improvement. It is worth repeating that those subjects which require good light will need to be moved closer to the window in winter, and those which prefer moderate brightness should be placed at a greater distance from windows in the summer. There is no substitute for personal observation and experience. Perhaps in the future, books will give details of light measurements and relative humidity, as well as temperature. A thermometer, hygrometer and light meter will then enable home gardeners to follow precise instructions, and the maintenance of a flourishing houseplant collection will have become an exact science, but until then . . .

Do's and Don'ts

Do apply fertilizer, in small amounts, when plants are growing.

Do keep plants above the minimum recommended temperature at all times.

Do keep plants tidy and remove dead leaves.

Do buy plants with a particular position in mind.

Do inspect plants regularly, looking for pests, disease or inferior growth.

Do keep the compost moist throughout the summer.

Don't water in winter until the compost is almost dry.

Don't feed plants in the winter.

Don't allow excessive warmth during dormancy.

Don't subject plants to scorching windowsills, especially foliage subjects.

Don't repot in autumn and winter.

PLANT PROBLEMS

Most of the disorders which afflict houseplants are due to incorrect cultivation and the stress caused by environmental factors. Yet it is inevitable that at some time there will be an invasion by insect pests and occasionally an infection by certain pathogens. Inevitably, conditions which protect plants will favour those creatures which make a living on them, and indeed sometimes will encourage disease organisms, but well-grown and robust plants should resist these attacks effectively.

The presence of disease must never be tolerated, but there are different attitudes about infestations of insect pests. Some gardeners will not be unduly perturbed about small populations, but others will feel that every single one should be eradicated. If total elimination is

Fig 113 Powdery mildew is not a very serious complaint, but if untreated it can spread from the leaves to stems and flowers.

favoured then routine spraying with an insecticide is almost unavoidable, but nowadays strong feelings are aroused by the use of toxic chemicals and alternative treatments are being sought by the horticultural industry. A few sprays are available based on insecticidal soap, and they are likely to increase in number as the 'green gardening' movement claims more adherents.

There has always been the physical option of finger and thumb or a wet sponge to remove harmful residents on plant foliage, and if practised on a regular basis it is most effective. However, the most important element − whatever the treatment − is early detection, and this is only accomplished by observation and frequent inspection of the plants, preferably with a magnifying glass.

When plants are ailing there is very great difficulty in identifying the cause because symptoms of pest attack can be similar or even identical to those brought about by inappropriate cultivation. Consequently, it is better to search carefully for intruders before considering the possibilities of over-feeding, over-watering or disorders caused by dry air or incorrect light levels. Having confirmed the presence of unwelcome visitors, action can be taken. Some pests breed at a phenomenal rate and whereas just a few will be harmless, a large infestation will cause visible damage and threaten the health of a plant.

Newcomers to plant care are often amazed that an apparently pristine plant has become laden with pests only a few days after it was purchased from the garden centre. Obviously it was maintained insect-free in the greenhouse in which it was grown, but these common creatures are truly formidable in their survival capability. Usually the eggs and often the larvae which precede the adult stage are immune to the effects of chemical treatment, and when in the warmth and safety of the home, the mature insects emerge unscathed and proceed to proliferate. Other species are carried by the wind and an open window gives them access to indoor plants, whilst some have excellent aerial ability and fly on a random reconnaissance until they find suitable vegetation on which to feed.

Diseases

The minute organisms which cause disease in plants are too numerous to contemplate. There are probably more than 1,600 kinds of bacteria, and possibly 100,000 species of fungi, not to mention the dozens of viruses which have been identified as harmful to plants. And then there are countless numbers which remain obscure and undiscovered. The classifications of disease organisms are of little importance to gardeners, but it is useful to know the enemy in general terms so that an appropriate response can be made. Almost without exception the bacterial infections and the viral diseases are not treatable because they are not susceptible to the otherwise impressive armoury of sophisticated chemicals. If plants are believed to be suffering from these pathogens they must be destroyed so that the possibility of infecting other plants is diminished. The disease will not be spread by leaf touching leaf, but by sap-feeding insects which will be discussed in the second part of this chapter.

That leaves us with fungi, but fortunately they can be discouraged by good cultivation and controlled by fungicidal sprays. Fungi are usually considered part of the plant kingdom yet because they lack the magic of chlorophyll, they cannot produce food in such a fundamental way. Instead they depend on other organisms for their nutrition which is obtained in three ways: from dead matter, from living tissue, and from a combination of living and dead material.

Most of the fungi which attack plants fall into the third category, which is why it is always important to remove dead or dying leaves and stems. Fungal spores are carried in the air and decaying leaves are an open invitation to them; the fungus develops and then infects the healthy parts of the host plant. The insidious nature of fungal complaints is that the plant tissue is invaded and will be destroyed progressively unless remedial action is taken promptly. Plant pathology is a vast and complex subject, and I make no apologies for reducing it to a few paragraphs because I believe that much gardening literature is preoccupied with what might go wrong. Disease is a major threat to commercial growers who might have thousands of the same species in one greenhouse, but for the amateur with a few plants in the home there are only a few ailments which are commonly encountered. If something unusual is suspected, diagnosis is extremely difficult and I would recommend that advice is sought from local authority experts, garden centres, local horticultural societies and the advisory services offered by the gardening press. That said, the most familiar and widespread complaints will almost certainly affect houseplants, especially those which are made more vulnerable by inferior cultivation or subjected to adverse conditions.

Botrytis

This scientific name is used rather loosely by the gardening fraternity to describe a multitude of fungal disorders and may otherwise be called grey mould, mildew or straightforward rot. It is prevalent in moist and overcrowded conditions, and its impact on terraria and bottle gardens can be devastating when it is not detected in its early stages. Typically, the symptoms are soft rotting of stems and leaves which later become covered with a soft, grey fungal growth, but the first signs are light-coloured spots on leaves and flowers.

Improved ventilation and additional warmth will inhibit further infection, but it is essential to remove as much affected vegetation as possible and a fungicidal spray should be used. The so-called systemic controls are the most effective, for as well as killing the fungus by contact, the chemical is absorbed into the plant itself and therefore 'immunizes' the cells against infection. When spraying the affected plant it is worthwhile treating others in close proximity.

Mildew

Another general name used for certain fungal diseases, but it is usually meant to signify two different types. Downy mildew is less common and more serious because it develops inside the plant, and the first signs may be nothing more than a yellowing of leaves and generally poor growth. Powdery mildew lives on the surfaces of leaves and stems and its name is accurately descriptive – small white spots may be an early indication before large areas become covered with the white powder. It spreads with alarming rapidity and, if unchecked, plants succumb completely and will often contaminate their neighbours.

Again, the removal of affected parts of the plant is imperative and then the use of a proprietary fungicide. These are not especially 'nasty' chemicals, but it is important to follow the instructions which are printed on the bottle. They will advise that fish bowls and aquaria should be covered if they are close to those plants which require treatment.

Crown and Stem Rot

This is yet another fungus which affects the base of plants and is frequently referred to as basal rot; it attacks at or just below soil level and the spread is such that the plant is quickly killed. If the trouble is caught early enough, remove all the rotten tissue and keep the plant warm and well ventilated, making sure that it is not watered until absolutely necessary. Otherwise, throw away the plant and compost and sterilize the pot.

Pests

There are a very large number of insects which will damage plants. The following list is confined to the most likely.

Aphids

More than 500 aphid species are found in Britain and northern Europe, and although they may be black, white, red, yellow and orange, as well as many shades in between, the term greenfly is popularly used for the whole spectrum. As

Fig 114 *A heavy infestation of aphids, as usual, on the uppermost parts of the plant and on buds. The severity of this attack could lead to distorted shoots and malformed flowers.*

Aphids prefer to congregate around the growing tips of plants or on the undersides of the uppermost leaves, and their presence is sometimes unobserved until white debris is seen around the base of the plant and a black residue is noticed on lower foliage. The debris is dead aphids, and the residue results from honeydew which is exuded by the insects frequently becoming contaminated by the growth of a sooty mould. Wiping the leaves with a soapy sponge will clean away the sticky deposit and will also eradicate the aphids, except where there is a large population. In this case an insecticide will be necessary, and the low toxicity sprays are effective or those which are based on insecticidal soap.

It should be emphasized that small numbers of greenfly will not damage plants but large colonies will stunt growth and cause distorted stems and leaves. Perhaps the main consideration though is the fact that these insects are the most important carriers of diseases from one plant to another.

individuals they are insignificant, but as a group of insects they are formidable and whilst our interest is in the plants which fall host to them, some facts about aphids are quite fascinating.

They are soft-bodied, sap-feeding insects and colonies often consist of winged and wingless types. Although, at best, they are poor fliers, they are widely dispersed by wind and air currents. It is, however, their reproductive talents which are most impressive and scientists have calculated that a single aphid, given 100 days of agreeable weather, could give rise to 10 million tons of aphids! Only one of these insects would be required for this incredible feat because most specimens are female, giving birth to live young, and the intervention of the male of the species is not needed. Fortunately, for plants and humans, this theoretical achievement is never realized because aphids are a major food source for many other insects and birds, and their numbers are severely depleted by unfavourable weather and many other factors.

Fig 115 *Whitefly accumulating on the underside of a* Chrysanthemum *leaf. It is the uppermost leaves and stems which are most attractive to sap-feeding insects.*

100

Whitefly

Apparently a sub-tropical species of this insect was accidentally introduced into European greenhouses and has now become widely established. They are like minute white moths which fly well, deposit honeydew, and their larvae feed on sap. Tomato growers are plagued by whitefly, which is also fond of some ornamental plants, with perhaps a preference for fuchsia and regal pelargoniums. Where these preferred plants are absent, others are readily infested.

Elimination is difficult and when sprays are used it must be realized that only the adults are killed; the eggs are not really affected. This means that spraying must be repeated every week until no further signs are seen.

Mealy Bugs

These can be a considerable nuisance because they inhabit parts of the plant which are hidden from view and can be difficult to reach by hand or spray. The bugs are small creatures dressed in a white fluffy material and are at home amidst a wide variety of plants. Their eradication is complicated by the fact that the offspring are cocooned in a waxy substance which is impervious to ordinary sprays. Small infestations can be cleared by using a cotton bud or small brush which has been soaked in methylated spirit.

Red Spider Mites

Apart from the fact that they are neither spiders nor particularly red, they are perhaps the major pest for plants in warm and dry situations. To see them is a test of vision because they are never more than 1mm(0.03in) long, but sometimes they do produce a white webbing which is evident between leaves and stems. An attack will result in light mottling and discolouration of leaves: when noticed this means there will be thousands of red spider mites present. Spraying plants with water will discourage the mites, but bad infestations can only be treated effectively with insecticides.

Root Mealy Bugs

Smaller but similar to their above-ground brethren and more difficult to detect, these bugs bring about the gradual deterioration of the afflicted plant. They can usually be seen around the roots if the plant pot is removed and they seem particularly fond of cacti and succulents. If their presence is suspected the compost should be drenched with a normal-strength solution of insecticide.

Scale Insects

These pests are like pale brown limpets on leaves and stems, but they are often overlooked on account of their small size and effective disguise. However, they also produce honeydew and if you find a sticky mess which is not due to whitefly or aphids, then detailed examination will probably reveal scale insects. Insecticides will control them and so too will swabbing with methylated or surgical spirits.

Sciarid Flies

The widespread use of peat-based potting composts have made this a common pest, and most people have seen the adults scurrying over the surface of the compost. They do no harm to plants but their maggots, which are white-bodied and black-headed, do feed on roots. Watering with insecticide is the most expedient remedy.

Vine Weevils

The adult beetles do eat pieces of foliage but they are rarely seen because of nocturnal habits and the fact that they are compost-coloured. Movement is very slow and is unlikely to catch your eye, but as a pest vine weevil has become one of the biggest threats to a wide range of pot plants. Perhaps the bugs first attacked vines, moving to cyclamen and begonia and subsequently even more plants. They literally inhabit corms and tubers, and wreak havoc amongst the roots of other plants. The grubs are immune to

Fig 116   The adult vine weevil eats pieces of foliage.

most treatments, but quite recently an effective remedy was found although it may never be available to amateur growers. Wilting is the first real sign of trouble, and by this time the creamy grubs have done such damage as to necessitate disposal of the plant.

Chemical Treatments

At the beginning of this section I mentioned the strong emotions which can be aroused when chemical sprays are discussed, and it will have been noticed that in each case of pest or disease the use of insecticide or fungicide has been included as at least the main option (and sometimes the only one). My own view is that amateurs should not spray as a regular routine, although a case could perhaps be made for fungicides because the problem may be well underway before it can be identified. With pesticides I only 'shoot on sight', and would not advocate a policy of using these chemicals before the enemy has been seen. However, this viewpoint cannot be extended to embrace commercial growers who would be courting total disaster by adopting such a policy. I am making this point

to reinforce the realization that practically all plants bought from nurseries and garden centres will have been sprayed regularly.

Considerable research has been and is being undertaken to find alternative treatments, and there have been some notable successes especially in the field of using parasites to destroy the offending insects. However, for diseases and a great majority of pests, there is no practical means of defeating the enemy without using chemicals which are sometimes highly toxic, requiring professional application and a great many safeguards. This should not be construed as an apology for commercial growers, but rather an explanation of something which I accept on the commercial level but do not heartily endorse for home gardeners. Some of the chemicals can only be used by experienced personnel and cannot be sold to the public, but even those which are judged to be relatively harmless to humans must be treated with respect and, I believe, used with the utmost restraint.

Incidentally, a few of the parasitic or predator remedies are available to the gardening public, but unfortunately their deployment is rarely successful for amateurs. They work much better on the large scale and the correct timing of the operation calls for some expertise, but for our purpose there is a more serious deficiency. When the predators have eaten all the pests they die out or go elsewhere; then the pests return but the predators do not – unless you buy some more. You may wish to try your own experiment in the greenhouse or even in a terrarium, but I am sure that you will find it expensive and largely ineffective. However, it is a very recent development and it may be that the future will see the introduction of techniques which are successful for gardeners and reasonably economic.

As a final word on the subject of maladies, I would urge you to buy plants which are pest- and disease-free and, if possible, scrutinize them well before taking them home. Fungi are without any saving graces, but you may find that many of the insects are exceedingly interesting and when seen under a magnifying glass quite startling!

CHAPTER 8

Home Propagation

I do not believe that everyone will want to propagate from their plants, but for many hobbyists it is the most satisfying achievement, and the diverse ways in which vegetation can reproduce itself are fascinating. It also appeals to those who appreciate getting 'new for old', and something for nothing is an attractive idea. Houseplants are expensive and if they can be rejuvenated or replaced without cost, so much the better, especially if there are no penalties for failure. Some equipment is essential and although not cheap the returns are good and there is the possibility of improvization.

Seeds and cuttings, which are the principle means of propagation, will be much more successful if constant warmth and humidity can be provided inside a plastic-topped, thermostatically, controlled, heated propagator. This ensures the maintenance of a predetermined temperature together with a moist atmosphere, independent of the surrounding conditions. The heat source in the base of the equipment is conducive to root formation, and the humidity prevents the cutting from losing moisture whilst the roots are growing. Seeds, too, need moist air as well as warm compost and, when germination has taken place, the seedlings benefit from the protected environment during the early stages of growth.

The improvization mentioned can take the form of a plant pot filled with compost, and at least three sticks inserted around the perimeter. An appropriately sized, clear plastic bag is then used to enclose the pot and the sticks provide the formation of a tent structure. This may sound rather 'Heath Robinson' but it is highly effective, satisfying the crucial requirement of a humid enclosure. It does not, however, provide additional warmth and therefore this technique is really confined to late spring and summer when temperatures are naturally higher. At other times the proximity of a radiator can be utilized, but remember that when central heating is off the temperature drops markedly, and this could be fatal to cuttings and seeds during the winter.

The majority of the plants which are listed in this book can be propagated successfully by one or more methods, and the appropriate technique is recommended in the summary table, but there are some subjects which defy enthusiasm and the amateur. Such plants need specialist equipment and, more importantly, expertise and professional experience; that is not to say that you should not try because you may just succeed.

THE NINE METHODS
Division

For the home cultivator this is the most basic and least demanding method. It can be used for plants which form clumps of growth as they develop. Some may produce stems as well as basal growth which gives a propagation option, but those without can only be propagated by division. The latter technique is used when a plant has become so large that it needs repotting. During this process examination will show where segments can be pulled or cut from the main growth. Cutting with a knife is usually preferable to pulling, but in either case it is important that the new piece is detached together with some roots. Spring or early summer is the

Fig 117   An African violet which has reached the stage where it can be divided to provide extra plants. It has formed three distinct clumps which can easily be teased apart.

Fig 118   The three 'new' plants are potted separately.

Fig 119   A mature Hippeastrum *bulb showing a leaf at the side which is growing from an offset below the surface. Two small offsets, which are small bulbs, are shown on the right.*

best time to divide plants so that ensuing growth will repair the damaged tissue quickly.

Offsets

Some subjects produce small shoots which are apparently separate from the main part of the plant, but in fact are attached under the surface of the compost. In some cases this juvenile growth comes from a bulbil which has formed next to the 'mother' bulb and the attachment is usually slight. Whether from bulb or basal shoot preserve as much as possible of the roots. The procedure is timely when active growth is under-way or just about to begin.

Ground Layering

Most climbing and trailing species can be in-creased in this way, and it is a reliable if some-

Fig 120   Ivies and other trailing plants can be propagated by ground layering. A shoot is 'pegged' into another pot and, when roots have formed, it can be severed from the parent plant.

times slow method. Leading shoots are pinned into the compost of an adjacent small pot using a V-shaped piece of wire or a hairpin. If a shallow cut is made in the stem, where it is touching the compost, the rooting process will often be accelerated but it is by no means essential. Ivies and vines are ideally suited to this technique, but any plants making flexible stems which can easily be bent into position will root in this way.

Air Layering

Plants which make thick stems are normally air layered, and it is an excellent means of getting a new plant when the old one has become too large or has deteriorated owing to the loss of lower leaves. Choose a point, not more than 30cm(1ft) from the tip of the plant, which is 2.5cm(1in) or so below a healthy leaf joint. Then use a sharp knife to cut part way through the stem and insert a matchstick or piece of plastic to

keep the incision open. Wrap 2.5cm(1in) above and below the cut with damp sphagnum moss, and cover the whole area with plastic film tying it top and bottom with string to keep the moss moist. This is a slow but fairly certain method, and when roots can be seen within the plastic cover the stem can be severed and the new plant potted up. An alternative to cutting the parent stem is carefully stripping about 13mm(0.5in) of bark around the circumference, and then using the same procedure to enclose the area. The major advantage of these layering techniques is that the potential new plant is sustained by the parent until roots have formed, no matter how long this may take.

Stem Cuttings

The majority of the subjects in the plant kingdom grow by means of stems and, in theory, all such species can be propagated by cutting off the top

Fig 121   Cuttings of Ficus pumila (creeping fig), which will root at most times of the year if kept warm and moist.

Fig 122 *Regal pelargonium cuttings are usually taken in the early autumn when they will root in about ten days.*

Fig 123 *This leaf from an African violet was inserted into the compost and after five or six weeks, a new plant is seen growing from the stalk.*

section and inserting it into suitable compost. Two or three pairs of leaves are left at the top of the cutting whilst the remainder are removed, and a clean cut is made just below one of the leaf nodes (where the leaf stalk joins the stem). The plant hormones which will promote root growth are more abundant at these junctions, but the cut end can be dipped into a rooting powder to further stimulate this activity. Hormone rooting powders also incorporate a fungicide which usefully protects against fungal attack where the interior plant tissue has been exposed. Cuttings are then pushed gently into a sandy compost and placed in a propagator or, as described earlier, into a plastic tent. The time taken for roots to form varies enormously depending on the subject, and can be several weeks, but a propagator with a heated base will certainly speed up the process. Timing is also important, and the general rule is that late spring and summer is ideal, although late summer and autumn is favoured for some plants such as geraniums.

Leaf Cuttings

The ability of plants to form roots from various parts of their anatomy is both incredible and immensely useful. Even more amazing are those plants which are readily propagated from mere leaves. *Gloxinia*, *Saintpaulia*, and several small-leaved *Peperomia* yield leaves with a stalk which, if inserted into compost, will form a new plant. On the other hand many succulent leaves are without stalks, but will nonetheless root if the cut end is placed into a suitable medium. The most curious of all leaf cuttings are those which can be taken from *Begonia rex*, *Streptocarpus* and *Sanseveiria* because sections of these leaves will root if they are inserted vertically into the compost. The first two will also root if leaf sections are placed flat on the compost because new plants form from the veins. It is therefore helpful if some of the veins are lightly cut on the underside before placing them in contact with the compost.

Cane Cuttings

Some plants which have thick stems, such as *Dieffenbachia* and *Dracaena*, reach a stage when they become an eyesore with most of the lower leaves lost. This is the time for courage, and instead of consigning the plant to the dustbin, an attempt can be made to achieve 'new for old'. It is wise to use the top section as a conventional cutting, but there is also the option of using the bare stem for a few cane cuttings. Cut the stem into 6.5cm(2.5in) segments, ensuring that each piece has at least one but preferably two leaf nodes, and place them horizontally on the compost. If you detect that leaf buds are swelling or are about to become active, they should be placed uppermost; alternatively, the pieces of cane can be inserted vertically, making sure that the buried portion is the lower part of the stem.

Ready-Made Plantlets

There are a few subjects which produce miniature offspring and the results are most convenient for the home cultivator. *Chlorophytum* bears plantlets at the ends of long stems, whilst *Tolmiea* uses mature leaves for the purpose, and the fern *Asplenium bulbiferum* has tiny plants on the tips of its fronds. *Saxifraga sarmentosa* does its best to justify the mother of thousands name, and another fascinating exponent of this kind of procreation is the succulent *Bryophyllum daigremontianum* which lines the edges of practically all its leaves with plantlets. It is so prolific that it has earned the title of good luck plant.

All these offspring, whether they have developed roots or not, should be pushed gently into compost and given the protection of a propagator until signs of new growth are evident.

All the methods of propagation so far described are vegetative reproduction, and the resultant plants are identical to the parents — with one exception. In some instances (such as mother in law's tongue) variegated plants revert to their all-green state when cuttings are taken. If you want

Fig 124 *Young plants and cuttings in an electrically heated propagator. This maintains a pre-set temperature and the transparent, plastic canopy (which has been removed) keeps the internal atmosphere moist.*

to propagate a variegated *Sansevieria* for example, the cuttings will lose the variegations, and division is the only way of achieving your aim.

The final word about cuttings, of all kinds, is that natural processes are not certain and it is wise to take more cuttings than you will need because some, and occasionally all, will fail. This may be because of inexperience or neglect, but then again experts have their share of bad luck. Such failures are inexplicable. Try again is the only answer, particularly where the subject is difficult, and preferably try at a different time of the year.

Seed

The sexual reproduction resulting in seeds means that the genetic characteristics of both parents

Fig 125   Heated propagators, thermometer and seed trays – the correct equipment will provide more chance of success.

are mixed, and although the offspring may closely resemble them they will be slightly but uniquely different. This has important repercussions for home gardeners who love to grow plants from pips or 'stones' because the results can be extremely variable. An orange pip, for example, may come from a superbly edible fruit but the resultant tree will almost certainly not be the same and may be grossly inferior in terms of its fruiting quality. Of course this does not detract from the pleasures of cultivating such seeds, but it will avoid disappointment if the point is understood.

Most of the plants featured in this book are propagated vegetatively, but a glance into any comprehensive seed catalogue shows that many popular species can be bought by the packet. Flowering subjects are dominant in this respect but there are quite a few foliage plants for which seed is available – *Aralia*, *Asparagus*, *Coffea* and *Ficus*, for instance. However, fairly high temperatures are normally needed for successful germination – over 21°C(70°F) – and in the case of *Coffea*, 29.5°C(85°F) is required, germination taking five or six weeks. This suggests that a heated propagator is essential, but I would not want to deter anyone from using the facility of an airing cupboard as long as expectations are not too high. A thermometer will be essential, preferably a maximum/minimum type, so that possible sites in the home can be tested for suitable germination areas. Armed with that information you can consult the catalogues for details about the required temperatures for the subjects of your choice.

Making recommendations about the various means of propagating plants tends to highlight the difficulties, but I must emphasize that without our levels of knowledge and with considerable disadvantages, the Victorian householders had great success. So too do many of our contemporaries who take advantage of the advice which assails them from books, magazines and television programmes. All are important sources of information and are instrumental in removing the myth and magic which envelopes many areas of horticulture, including propagation.

It may help to realize that seeds 'want' to germinate, and cuttings are disposed to strike. In the case of seeds they have been programmed by millions of years of evolution, and they are stimulated into activity by moisture and the right temperature range. Leaves and stems which have been severed from a plant will cling on to life by taking up as much water as is possible without roots, and will endeavour to repair the damaged tissue and reinstate their missing parts. In this case the gardener's role is to provide a water-laden atmosphere around the cutting which greatly reduces transpiration, and allows it to survive long enough to be able to regenerate a rooting system. In both these examples the gardener does not have to do anything except provide the right conditions for the natural processes to progress.

Having served as propagandist for home plant propagation I must also point out that most of the species which are featured in this book are tropical or semi-tropical, and some are propagated only with the greatest difficulty. Others need but a nod and a wink before they multiply, and the only problem is finding a home for the ensuing plants. The best parallel I can think of in the animal kingdom is a comparison between the fecundity of rabbits and the reluctance of pandas to breed in captivity; and don't forget that houseplants are away from their natural environment and are in a real sense captive. Anyone contemplating a breeding programme for those animals would be wise to start with the rabbits and use the experience gained for the more ambitious project. The same is true for the propagation of plants, and I hope that the plant summary tables will enable you to identify which are the rabbits and the pandas.

CHAPTER 9

Seeing and Buying Houseplants

Today, a large proportion of houseplant sales are through supermarket chains and the DIY multiples. Clearly, these outlets have no special interest in plants as such, and very few would claim to offer information about what they sell and how to care for it. Inevitably, the range of plants is confined to the most popular subjects and there is little incentive for them to increase the varieties on offer. Nevertheless, they have a profound influence on the houseplant industry because their huge purchasing power enables them to determine what plants are grown, how big they should be, the size of the pot and, most importantly, what the price will be.

I have said elsewhere that houseplants are expensive and, to the customer, this may seem the case, but the growers are painfully aware that prices have remained fairly static throughout the last decade. In all parts of horticulture it is the growers who supply the expertise and suffer the risks, but their financial returns are marginal, whilst the retailers get the larger profits. When labour and fuel costs are considered, as well as the often huge capital investment in greenhouses, houseplants are relatively cheap. It could be argued that growers should get a better return but the power of the major retailers is such that they will probably always be able to dictate terms. Many houseplant sales take place in garden centres and nurseries and they have considerable advantages over the multiples as far as the plants are concerned. There are greenhouses to display the plants but, more significantly, the environmental conditions and trained staff are able to ensure that the plants have a much longer shelf life. Supermarkets are handicapped by inadequate natural light, excess warmth and dryness, and staff who are not usually trained in the care of plants.

The rapid growth in houseplant sales during the 1980s was clearly due to the multiple retailers, but they attracted considerable criticism from within and without the horticultural industry because plants had often deteriorated before they were sold. Organizations pointed to a fall in standards and were also concerned about price variations and, especially, the lack of proper labelling. I have encountered, within the industry, the opinion that detailed information on plant labels is a deterrent to sales which has resulted in frequent examples which border on the disgraceful. Some merely categorize plants as 'flowering' or 'foliage', without naming them and I take this as an insult to consumers. Others may indicate a general type, such as 'fern'. I believe that all plants should be specifically named and that the information about cultivation should be as comprehensive as space will allow. Most gardeners like to know about their purchases and should know precisely what they have bought and how to care for it; those who want to ignore the information are free to do so.

The new horticultural age is with us to the extent that there are many greenhouse complexes which have computer controlled temperature, humidity, ventilation, feeding and watering. As in the case of old farming methods, labour costs are still the major factor, but new machinery is now available which can prick out seedlings and pot up larger plants at the rate of thousands per hour. This, too, implies further specialization because these robot horticulturalists are designed to deal with uniform sizes. Further futuristic developments are inevitable, but even now there is a new generation of houseplants which is virtually untouched by the hands of humans.

HOUSEPLANTS ON VIEW

Every garden centre has a houseplant section, but whilst some have quite a good selection, others have very few and not many of these establishments display their goods with any degree of imagination. There are, however, exceptions.

My dream is for the establishment of two or three suitably sited centres in each country which would display, in an attractive way, all the houseplants commercially obtainable. There would also be an advice bureau to distribute informational leaflets, and a list of sources for all the plants on show. This would be immensely helpful to the consumer and would also be an effective shop window for the promotion of indoor plants. Alternatively, a few annual shows for the public would be better than nothing, but sadly these ideas are likely to remain fantasies because they would require the kind of cooperative effort which is rare in horticultural industries of most countries.

OBTAINING PLANTS

Those who are looking for an introduction to houseplants will have no difficulty in buying good plants at reasonable prices, and although garden centres maintain their plants in better condition the situation is improving with other outlets. One major supermarket chain in Britain pioneered a sell-by date policy for houseplants, and it seems likely that similar retail outlets will progressively adopt better systems of quality control. If you can identify a good retailer with good quality and a fairly wide choice, then take your business there because you won't do better. My preference is to buy from growers, but nowadays this is hardly an option. 'To grow is to know', but economic realities mean that only a few specialists actually grow what they sell and, for instance, there are not many garden centres which raise even a proportion of the plants they offer; they are mostly plant supermarkets. That said, it is normally possible to get some advice from garden centre staff about the plants of your choice.

On the other hand, those home gardeners who wish to extend the range of plants which they grow may need to contact specialist nurseries and societies. This is an excellent way of building up a distinguished, wide-ranging collection of plants.

SOMETHING NEW

There are many hundreds of different species in cultivation as houseplants but of these, only a small percentage are available commercially and they are the ones which have proved to be readily saleable. The main concentration has been on pot chrysanthemums, African violets, begonias, geraniums and busy Lizzie (patient Lucy) as flowering subjects, with cacti, succulents, spider plants and ivies as the main foliage contenders. In contrast with garden plants, especially bedding subjects, very few houseplants have occupied the attention of plant breeders and consequently there is a fairly narrow range from which to choose. Economic considerations are, of course, paramount and therefore the only way of procuring unusual subjects is to contact the small-scale, specialist producers or to find amateur enthusiasts. Happily there are occasional exceptions to this general rule and one such has occured in recent years.

A plant was discovered in Chihuahua, Mexico in 1972 which may become a future best-seller. It was named *Tacitus bellus* and naturally is known

Fig 126 Tacitus bellus, *known as the Chihuahua plant.*

as the Chihuahua flower. Star-shaped blooms in a magenta pink are produced in great profusion and cover the plant for some weeks and the grey-green leaves are also an attraction. *Tacitus* is a succulent and should be immune to the ravages of dry air. It is reasonably available in North America and some plants have reached the United Kingdom market, but it may take a few more years before it has the opportunity to achieve popularity. Seed is obtainable from a few sources and as I write there is some in my propagator although I believe it will be twelve months before flowering size is reached (*see* Fig 126).

SOMETHING NEWER

I have, for many years, been trialling garden subjects as houseplants with a particular emphasis on compact flowering plants, but there is one which I am presently assessing which has possibilities as a foliage specimen. *Houttuynia cordata* 'Variegata' is a marsh plant from the Far East which relishes cool moist conditions and can be quite invasive in the garden. The leaves are green variegated with yellow and red and give off a pleasant orange aroma, and white flowers with green centres are produced in summer. The plant is deciduous and a hardy perennial, but I am not sure that it would remain attractive under room conditions.

IN CONCLUSION

There is the view that houseplants are inexpensive consumables and should not be expected to have a lifespan beyond three or four weeks. I have no wish to deter anyone from gaining pleasure from this short-term philosophy, but my belief is that it misses the whole point of cultivation. If interior decoration were the only motivation for housing plants, we would be entirely satisfied with silk flowers and plastic foliage, but this is clearly not so. The fascination in growing is that the subjects are alive and to keep them that way is a natural

Fig 127 Cuttings of a plant which, as far as I am aware, has not been tried as an indoor subject. It is Houttuynia *whose natural habitat is in wet soils. It should be resistant to over-watering, but I am uncertain about the ability of its handsome foliage to withstand dry air.*

and even instinctive ambition. It does mean that they are decorative for longer, but the greater significance is the sense of reward and fulfilment when plants are successfully sustained.

To this end, there is no substitute for 'knowing' your plants and this implies the acquisition of experience and other kinds of knowledge. Initial failure is not inevitable, but when it occurs, there is an understandable sag in enthusiasm and the value of experience is often foreshortened. The best way to avoid this situation is to concentrate on the best 'survivors' and to ensure that plants are purchased with a particular site in mind. For those who have never tried, I heartily recommend the use of glass enclosures. The provision of a 'flora friendly' environment will virtually guarantee that plant obituaries are a thing of the past.

Whatever and however you cultivate, may your plants flourish and bring you joy and enormous satisfaction. I must, however, make a final plea about your watering can . . . it is impossible to make it redundant — but do confine it to seasonal employment and pension it off in the winter.

Appendices

I PLANT SUMMARY TABLES

Notes

Height – naturally, the ultimate height of plants will depend on conditions and cultivation and therefore the figure
   given is only a guide. This is especially true where climbers are involved, whose size can be limited by
   pruning. The + sign indicates that the subject can grow much taller.

Type – Flo describes a flowering plant.
   Fol describes a foliage plant.

Temperature – Cool is between 4.5–7.5°C(40–45°F). Moderate is 7.5–13°C(45–55°F). Warm is 13–16°C(55–60°F).
   These ranges are the minimum which should prevail.

Light – S   describes a position which receives some sunshine.
   B   the brightest place without direct sunshine.
   PS partial shade, where the brightness is more variable.
   Sh shady places away from windows but not murky corners.

Humidity – High humidity implies conditions which prevail in terraria and bottles.
   Moderate humidity can be provided by a gravel tray.
   Low humidity can be provided by 'normal' room conditions.
   Where a hygrometer reading is used – High is above 70 per cent
                                                             Moderate is 40–70 per cent
                                                             Low is below 40 per cent

Propagation – indicates the favoured method of producing new plants and detailed information is given in the
   propagation chapter. Where seed is an option, this is available for at least some of the species. The
   letters E, FE and D indicate the relative difficulty of propagation.
   E   – Easy. Seeds which germinate and cuttings which root quickly. All division is 'easy' but plants
         will need a period of intensive care.
   FE – Fairly easy. Cuttings and seeds may take longer to be successful.
   D – Difficult. Some plants in this category will present extreme propagation problems and may
         prove impossible in ordinary circumstances.

	Height	Type	Temp	Light	Humidity	Propagation
Abutilon	1.1m (45in)	Flo/Fol	Mod	PS	Mod	E Stemcuts/Seed
Achimenes	30cm (12in)	Flo	Warm	B	Mod	E Rhizomes/Seed
Acorus gramineus 'Pusillus'	10cm (4in)	Grass	Cool	B/PS	Mod	E Division
Acorus gramineus 'Variegatus'	38cm (15in)	Grass	Cool	B/PS	Mod	E Division
Adiantum hispidulum	38cm (15in)	Fern	Warm	B/PS	High	FE Division
Adiantum raddianum	30cm (12in)	Fern	Warm	B/PS	High	FE Division
Aechmea fasciata	45cm (18in)	Flo/Fol	Warm	B	Mod	FE Offsets
Agave americana 'Mediopicta'	30cm (12in)	Fol	Cool	S/B	Low	FE Leafcuts/Seed
Aglaonema	38cm (15in+)	Fol	Warm	B/PS	Mod	D Division

	Height	Type	Temp	Light	Humidity	Propagation
Allamanda	38cm (15in+)	Flo/Fol	Warm	B	High	FE Seed
Aloe variegata	25cm (10in)	Fol	Cool	S/B	Low	FE Leafcut/Seed
Ananas	45cm (18in)	Fol	Mod	S/B	Mod	E Offsets
Anthurium crystallinum	30cm (12in)	Fol	Warm	B	High	FE Division
Anthurium scherzerianum	38cm (15in)	Flo/Fol	Warm	B	High	FE Division
Aphelandra	25cm (10in)	Flo/Fol	Mod	B	Mod	FF Stemcuts
Araucaria	1.2m (48in+)	Tree	Cool	B/PS	Mod	D Seed
Asparagus	30cm (12in)	Fern (like)	Mod	B/PS	Mod	E Seed/Division
Aspidistra	60cm (24in)	Fol	Cool	PS/Sh	Low	FE Division
Asplenium	38cm (15in)	Fern	Mod	B/PS	High	FE Division
Aucuba	38cm (15in+)	Fol	Cool	B/Sh	Mod	E Stemcuts/Seed
Azalea indica	45cm (18in)	Flo	Cool	B	Mod	D Stemcuts
Begonia (other flowering types)	25cm (10in)	Flo	Mod	B	Mod	E Stemcuts
Begonia rex (and foliage types)	25cm (10in)	Fol	Warm	B	High	D Leafcuts/*rex* − Seed
Begonia semperflorens, 'Reiger', and 'Elatior'	30cm (12in)	Flo	Mod	B	Mod	E Stemcuts/Seed
Beloperone	20cm (8in)	Flo	Cool	S/B	Mod	E Stemcuts/Seed
Billbergia	30cm (12in)	Flo/Fol	Mod	B	Mod	FE Division
Blechnum	38cm (15in+)	Fern	Mod	B/PS	High	FE Division
Bougainvillea	30cm (12in+)	Flo	Cool	S	Low	D Stemcuts
Browallia	25cm (10in)	Flo	Mod	S/B	Mod	E Seed
Brunfelsia	45cm (18in)	Flo	Mod	B	Mod	D Stemcuts/Seed
Caladium	60cm (24in)	Fol	Warm	B/PS	High	D Offsets
Calathea	45cm (18in)	Fol	Warm	PS	High	D Division
Callisia (see *Tradescantia*)	15cm (6in)	Fol	Mod	B/PS	Mod	E Stemcuts
Callistemon	60cm (24in+)	Flo	Cool	S/B	Low	D Stemcuts/Seed
Campanula isophylla	15cm (6in)	Flo	Cool	B	Mod	FE Stemcuts/Seed
Carex	38cm (15in)	Grass	Cool	B/PS	Mod	E Division/Seed
Catharanthus	20cm (8in)	Flo	Mod	B	Mod	FE Seed
Celosia	25cm (10in)	Flo	Mod	S/B	Mod	E Seed
Ceterach	25cm (10in)	Fern	Warm	B/PS	High	FE Division
Chamaerops	76cm (30in+)	Palm	Mod	PS	Mod	D Seed
Chlorophytum	30cm (12in)	Grass	Cool	B/PS	Mod	E Plantlets
Chrysanthemum (Pot-mums)	30cm (12in)	Flo	Cool	B	Mod	− Not practicable
Cissus antarctica	30cm (12in)	Fol	Cool	B/PS	Mod	E Stemcuts/Seed
Cissus discolour	30cm (12in+)	Fol	Warm	PS	High	D Stemcuts
Citrus	60cm (24in)	Tree	Mod	S/B	Mod	D Stemcuts
Clerodendrum	60cm (24in+)	Flo/Fol	Mod	B	Mod	D Stemcuts
Clivia	50cm (20in)	Flo	Cool	B/PS	Mod	E Offsets (hybrids from seed)
Cocos	90cm (36in+)	Palm	Mod	PS	Mod	D Seed
Codiaeum	50cm (20in)	Fol	Warm	B	High	D Stemcuts
Coffea	60cm (24in+)	Fol	Mod	B	Mod	D Stemcuts/Seed
Columnea	25cm (10in)	Flo	Mod	B	Mod	D Stemcuts
Crassula	30cm (12in)	Fol	Mod	S/B	Low	E Stem/Leafcuts
Crossandra	38cm (15in)	Flo	Mod	B	High	D Stemcuts/Seed
Cryptanthus	15cm (6in)	Fol	Mod	B	Mod	D Offsets
Ctenanthe	60cm (24in)	Fol	Warm	PS	High	D Division
Cuphea	25cm (10in)	Flo	Cool	S/B	Low	E Stemcuts/Seed

	Height	Type	Temp	Light	Humidity	Propagation
Cyanotis (see *Tradescantia*)	15cm (6in)	Fol	Mod	PS	Mod	E Stemcuts
Cyclamen	30cm (12in)	Flo	Cool	B	Mod	FE Seed
Cyperus diffusus	38cm (12in)	Fol	Mod	PS/Sh	High	E Division
Cyrtomium	38cm (12in)	Fern	Mod	PS	Mod	FE Division/Seed
Davallia	30cm (12in)	Fern	Warm	B/PS	Mod	FE Division
Dieffenbachia	45cm (18in)	Fol	Warm	B/PS	Mod	FE Canecuts
Dipladenia	60cm (24in+)	Flo	Mod	B/PS	Mod	D Stemcuts
Dizyogotheca	38cm (15in)	Fol	Warm	B	High	D Stemcuts/Seed
Dracaena draco/godseffiana	60cm (24in)	Fol	Mod	PS	Low	FE Canecuts
Dracaena marginata/fragrans	90cm (36in)	Fol	Mod	Sh	Mod	FE Canecuts
Dracaena terminalis/sanderiana	60cm (24in)	Fol	Mod	PS	High	FE Canecuts
Epiphyllum	30cm (12in+)	Flo	Warm	B	Mod	E Stemcuts/Seed
Episcia cupreata	15cm (6in)	Flo/Fol	Mod	B	High	D Ground layer
Erica gracilis	25cm (10in)	Flo	Cool	S/B	Mod	D Stemcuts
Eucalyptus	1.5m (60in)	Tree	Cool	S/B	Low	E Seeds
Euonymus	38cm (15in)	Fol	Cool	S/B	Low	FE Stemcuts
Eustoma	38cm (15in)	Flo	Mod	S/B	Low	FE Seed
Exacum	15cm (6in)	Flo	Mod	B	Mod	E Seed
Fatshedera	30cm (12in+)	Fol	Mod	B/PS	Mod	E Stemcuts
Fatsia	25cm (10in)	Fol	Cool	B/PS	Mod	E Stemcuts/Seed
Ficus benjamina	1.5m (60in+)	Tree	Mod	B	Mod	FE Stemcuts/Seed
Ficus elastica	90cm (36in+)	Fol	Mod	PS	Mod	FE Air layer/Seed
Ficus pumila	10cm (4in)	Fol	Mod	B	High	E Stemcuts
Fittonia	10cm (4in)	Fol	Warm	PS	High	E Ground layer/ Stemcuts/Division
Fuchsia	30cm (12in)	Flo	Mod	B/PS	Mod	E Stemcuts
Grevillea	1.2m (48in+)	Tree	Cool	B	Mod	E Seed
Gynura	15cm (6in+)	Fol	Mod	B	Mod	E Stemcuts
Hedera	15cm (6in)	Fol	Cool	B	Mod	E Stemcuts
Heliotropium	25cm (10in)	Flo	Cool	S/B	Mod	E Stemcuts/Seed
Helxine	7.5cm (3in)	Fol	Cool	B/PS	Mod	E Division
Heptapleurum	90cm (36in+)	Fol	Warm	B	Mod	FE Stemcuts
Hibiscus rosa-sinensis	30cm (12in+)	Flo	Mod	S/B	Mod	FE Stemcuts
Hippeastrum	38cm (15in)	Flo	Warm	S/B	Mod	FE Offsets/Seed
Howea	90cm (36in+)	Palm	Cool	PS	Mod	D Seed
Hoya	30cm (12in+)	Flo	Mod	S/B	Mod	FE Stemcuts
Hydrangea	38cm (15in+)	Flo	Cool	B	Humidity	E Stemcuts
Hypocyrta	30cm (12in)	Flo	Mod	B/PS	Mod	FE Stemcuts
Hypoestes	20cm (8in)	Fol	Mod	B	Mod	E Stemcuts/Seed
Impatiens	30cm (12in)	Flo	Mod	B/PS	Mod	E Stemcuts/Seed
Iresine	30cm (12in)	Fol	Mod	S/B	Mod	E Stemcuts
Kalanchoe	20cm (8in)	Flo	Mod	B	Low	FE Stemcuts/Seed
Lachenalia	20cm (8in)	Flo/Fol	Cool	S/B	Mod	E Offsets/Seed
Lantana	30cm (12in+)	Flo	Mod	S/B	Low	FE Stemcuts/Seed

	Height	Type	Temp	Light	Humidity	Propagation
Maranta	20cm (8in)	Fol	Warm	PS	Mod	FE Division
Mimosa	25cm (10in)	Fol	Mod	S/B	Mod	FE Seed
Monstera	1.2m (48in)	Fol	Mod	PS	Mod	FE Air layer/Seed
Neanthe bella	45cm (18in)	Palm	Cool	PS/Sh	Low	D Seed
Nephrolepsis	30cm (12in)	Fern	Mod	B/PS	Mod	FE Division
Nertera	15cm (6in)	Flo	Cool	S/B	Mod	E Division/Seed
Pachystachys	25cm (10in)	Flo	Mod	B	Mod	E Stemcuts
Passiflora	38cm (15in)	Flo	Cool	S/B	Mod	FE Stemcuts/Seed
Pelargonium	30cm (12in)	Flo	Cool	S	Low	E Stemcuts/Seed
Pellaea	15cm (6in)	Fern	Mod	B/PS	Mod	FE Division/Seed
Pentas	30cm (12in)	Flo	Mod	S/B	Mod	FE Stemcuts
Peperomia	15cm (6in)	Fol	Mod	B/PS	Mod	E Stem and leafcuts
Philodendron melanochryson	38cm (15in)	Fol	Warm	B/PS	Mod	FE Stemcuts/Air layer
Philodendron scandens (and others)	38cm (15in+)	Fol	Mod	PS/Sh	Mod	FE Stemcuts/Air layer/ Seed
Phyllitis	30cm (12in)	Fern	Mod	B/PS	Mod	FE Division
Pilea	10cm (4in)	Fol	Mod	B/PS	Mod	E Stemcuts/Seed
Plectranthus	20cm (8in)	Fol	Mod	B/PS	Low	E Stemcuts
Pleomele	30cm (12in)	Fol	Mod	PS	Mod	D Canecuts
Plumbago	60cm (24in)	Flo	Cool	S/B	Mod	FE Stemcuts/Seed
Podocarpus	45cm (18in)	Tree	Cool	S/B	Mod	D Stemcuts
Polyscias	25cm (10in)	Fol	Warm	B/PS	Mod	D Stemcuts
Polystichum	20cm (8in)	Fern	Mod	B/PS	Mod	FE Division
Primula	25cm (10in)	Flo	Cool	B/PS	Mod	FE Seed/Division
Pteris	20cm (8in)	Fern	Mod	B/PS	Mod	FE Division/Seed
Radermachera	90cm (36in)	Fol	Cool	B/PS	Low	FE Stemcuts/Seed
Rhoeo	38cm (15in)	Fol	Mod	B/PS	Mod	D Division/Seed
Rhoicissus	38cm (15in)	Fol	Cool	B/PS	Mod	E Stemcuts/Seed
Ruellia	60cm (24in)	Flo	Mod	S/B	Mod	FE Stemcuts
Saintpaulia	15cm (6in)	Flo	Warm	B	High	FE Division/Leafcuts/ Seed
Salpiglossis	25cm (10in)	Flo	Mod	S/B	Mod	FE Seed
Sanseveiria	60cm (24in)	Fol	Mod	B/PS	Low	FE Leafcut/ Division
Saxifraga	7.5cm (3in)	Fol	Cool	B	Mod	E Plantlets
Schefflera	90cm (36in)	Fol	Mod	B/PS	Mod	D Seed/Stemcuts
Schizanthus	38cm (15in)	Flo	Cool	S/B	Mod	E Seed
Schizocentron	30cm (12in)	Flo	Mod	S/B	Mod	D Stemcuts
Scindapsus	60cm (24in)	Fol	Mod	B/PS	Mod	D Stemcuts
Selaginella	7.5cm (3in)	Fol	Mod	PS	High	E Stemcuts/ Ground layer
Setceresia	25cm (10in)	Fol	Mod	B/PS	Mod	E Stemcuts
Siderasis	15cm (6in)	Fol	Warm	PS	High	FE Division
Sinningia	20cm (8in)	Flo	Warm	B	High	FE Leafcut/Seed
Smithiana	25cm (10in)	Flo	Warm	B	High	E Division
Spathyphyllum	45cm (18in)	Flo	Mod	B/PS	High	FE Division
Sprekelia	25cm (10in)	Flo	Cool	S/B	Mod	FE Offsets
Stephanotis	38cm (15in)	Flo	Warm	B	Mod	D Stemcuts/Seed
Streptocarpus	20cm (8in)	Flo	Mod	B	Mod	FE Leafcut/Division/ Seed

	Height	Type	Temp	Light	Humidity	Propagation
Strobilanthes	30cm (12in)	Fol	Mod	B/PS	Mod	FE Stemcuts
Syngonium	45cm (18in)	Fol	Mod	B/PS	Mod	FE Stemcuts/Seed
Thunbergia	38cm (15in)	Flo	Mod	S/B	Mod	E Seed
Tolmiea	20cm (8in)	Fol	Cool	B/PS	Mod	E Plantlets/Seed
Torenia	20cm (8in)	Flo	Mod	S/B	Mod	FE Seed
Tradescantia	15cm (6in)	Fol	Mod	B/PS	Mod	E Stemcuts
Vallota	38cm (15in)	Flo	Mod	S/B	Mod	E Offsets
Yucca	60cm (24in)	Fol	Cool	S/B	Low	FE Offsets/Seed
Zebrina	15cm (6in)	Fol	Mod	B/PS	Mod	E Stemcuts

II USEFUL ADDRESSES

United Kingdom

British Fern Society,
42 Lewisham Road,
Smethwick,
West Midlands,
B66 2BS.

The Saintpaulia and Houseplant Society
Miss Tanburn (Secretary),
82 Rossmore Court,
Park Road,
London NW1 6XY.

National Plant Collections

Adiantum
National Trust,
Tatton Park,
Knutsford,
Cheshire.

Asplenium
National Trust,
Sizergh Castle,
Kendal,
Cumbria.

Begonia (non-tuberous)
Glasgow Botanic Garden,
Glasgow.

Calathea
Calderstone Park,
Liverpool.

Passiflora
Greenholm Nurseries,
Kingston Seymour,
Clevedon,
Avon.

Yucca
Somerset College of Agriculture,
Bridgwater,
Somerset.

Houseplant Sources

African Violet Centre,
Station Road,
Terrington St. Clement,
King's Lynn,
Norfolk.

Anmore Exotics,
The George Staunton Estate,
Petersfield Road,
Havant,
Hampshire.
(Tropical foliage plant specialists.)

Bridgemere Garden World,
Bridgemere,
Cheshire.
(General houseplants: no mail order.)

Efenechtyd Nurseries,
Llanelidan,
Ruthin,
Clwyd.
(*Streptocarpus*, *Columnea* and other
    gesneriads.)

J. and D. Marston,
Culag,
Green Lane,
Nafferton,
Driffield,
East Yorkshire.
(Tender ferns.)

The Palm Farm,
Thornton Hall Gardens,
Thornton Cyrtis,
Near Ulceby,
South Humberside.

The Palm Centre,
22 Guildford Road,
London SW8 2BX.

The Torbay Palm Farm,
St. Marychurch Road,
Coffinswell,
Newton Abbott,
Devon.

Orchids

British Orchid Council,
20 Newbury Drive,
Davyhulme,
Manchester M31.

British Orchid Growers' Association,
2 Golvers Hill Road,
Kingsteignton,
Newton Abbott,
Devon.

Lighting

The Farm Electric Centre,
National Agriculture Centre,
Stoneleigh,
Kenilworth,
Warwickshire.
(They are pleased to send information to
    amateur growers.)

Goldenlite,
43 Halifax Road,
Staincliffe,
Dewsbury,
West Yorkshire.

Interpret Ltd,
Vincent Lane,
Dorking,
Surrey.

Canada

The African Violet Society of Canada,
1573 Arbordale Avenue,
Victoria BC,
V8N 5J1.

Houseplant Forum,
Horticom Inc,
PO Box 128,
Radisson WI 54867–D128.

Les Violettes Natalia,
124 Ch. Grapes,
Sawyerville QC J0B 3AO.

United States

African Violet Society of America,
PO Box 3609,
Beaumont,
TX 77704.

American Fern Society,
Milwaukee Public Museum,
800 W Wells Street,
Milwaukee,
WI 53233.

American Gloxinia and Gesneriad Society,
290 Federal Street,
Belchertown,
MA 01007.

Hobby Greenhouse Association,
8 Glen Terrace,
Bedford,
MA 01730.

The Indoor Gardening Society of America,
128 West 58th Street,
New York,
NT 10019.

The Peperomia Society,
249 Lexington Road,
Concord,
MA 01742.

Saintpaulia International,
1650 Cherry Hill Road South,
State College,
PA 16803.

Houseplant Sources

Indoor Gardening Supplies,
PO Box 40567AG,
Detroit,
MI 48240.

Lauray of Salisbury,
432 Undermountain Road,
Salisbury,
CT 06068.

Peter Paul's Nurseries,
Canandaigna,
NY 14424.

Sunshine State Topicals,
PO Box 1033,
Port Richley,
FL 34673–1033.

Tiki Nursery,
PO Box 187,
Fairview,
NC 28730.

Unusual Plants,
10065 River Mist Way,
Rancho Cordova,
CA 95670.

Australia

The African Violet Society of Australia,
53 Kibo Road,
Regents Park,
NSW 2143.

III NOMENCLATURE

Before the eighteenth century, the classification of plants was in a state of considerable confusion until a Swedish botanist proposed a system which grouped together plants which showed similarity of their flower make-up. Carl Linné set out the principles of his new system in 1737, and the binomial method which he formulated has been accepted world-wide. He was honoured by the award of a Latin name – Carolus Linnaeus.

Basically, the botanical name consists of two parts: the first name is the genus (plural genera) which groups together those plants which are fundamentally similar. The different plants within a genus are called species and this part of the name often describes a principal characteristic of the plant. Sometimes there is a third name which distinguishes between species which have different forms but which are not sufficiently different to be classed as separate species.

For example:

Sansevieria – the name of the genus, which could be described as the 'surname'.
hahnii – the name of the species (or christian name).
variegata – the name of a closely related variety.

The plant used as an example is therefore named *Sansevieria hahnii variegata*.

If the third name is in Latin, this almost always signifies that the variety originated in the wild. Those varieties which are the result of plant breeding are known as cultivars (cultivated varieties), or named varieties, for example, *Pelargonium domesticum* 'Aztec'. The cultivar name is not normally in Latin.

The family name is one of the major groupings of plants and consists of genera which have basically similar flower formation. Examples used in this book are Gesneriaceae, the gesneriads, and Araceae, the aroids.

The use of botanical names is a source of irritation to many gardeners and there is no doubt that the use of popular names is widespread and much favoured, especially by newcomers to the cultivation of plants. However, common names are most imprecise and cause particular difficulties where there is a language difference, but even when the language is shared, various names are used in different countries. The name *Impatiens* is universal but this plant is popularly called patient Lucy in the United States and busy Lizzy in the United Kingdom. A further complication arises where a popular name is used for more than one plant, and this is certainly the case with the umbrella plant and wandering jew. Consequently the emphasis in this book is on the use of scientific names with the addition of popular names where these are widely used and accepted.

IV GLOSSARY

I have endeavoured to use a minimum of technical terms and horticultural jargon in writing this book but the inclusion of a glossary is to explain some words which may be unfamiliar to inexperienced gardeners. Many people are introduced by horticulture by the cultivation of houseplants, and therefore some terms are listed for general guidance although they have not been used in the text.

Acid Medium A soil or compost which contains little or no lime.
Aerial Root Roots which grow from the stem above ground level, for example, those seen commonly on plants such as *Monstera* and *Philodendron*.
Air Layering A method of propagation (*see* Chapter 8).
Annual A plant which completes its life cycle within one year.
Aquatic Living wholly or partly in water.
Aroid Members of the Araceae family which include many popular houseplants – *Caladium*, *Monstera*, *Philodendron*, *Aglaonema*, *Anthurium* and *Dieffenbachia*.
Axil The angle where a leaf or leaf stalk joins a stem. A flower bud or growth bud often appears at the axil.

Bedding Plant One which is used for a temporary display. Many of these plants also perform well in pots.

Bicolour A flower having petals which bear two colours.

Biennial A plant which grows from seed, over-winters and then flowers and dies in the next year.

Blind Describes the condition where a growing point does not develop.

Bract A modified leaf, usually colourful, which is often mistaken for a petal. Plants with attractive bracts include *Poinsettia*, *Bougainvillea* and *Beloperone*.

Break The development of side shoots either naturally or after the growing tip of the plant has been removed.

Bulb An underground swollen bud which stores food and enables some plants to live during their dormant phase.

Bulbil A small bulb which usually grows from the base of a 'mother' bulb.

Compost For the houseplant grower this refers to a potting mixture which is made from peat, known as a soil-less compost, or one which comprises sterilized soil and which is called a loam compost. Confusion arises because this term is also used to describe decomposed plant material in the garden.

Corm A swollen plant stem which is often referred to quite wrongly as a bulb but it serves the same purpose.

Crown The part of a plant where the roots meet the growing shoots.

Cultivar A cultivated variety of a plant which has been bred in cultivation and has not occured in the wild. Sometimes called a named variety.

Cutting A part of a plant which can be root, leaf or stem, used to produce a new plant.

Dead-heading The removal of dead or dying flower heads.

Deciduous A plant which loses its leaves at the end of the growing season.

Division The means of propagating plants by dividing it into pieces. See chapter 7.

Dormant When a plant temporarily ceases growth; usually but not always in winter.

Double This describes a flower which has more than a single layer of petals.

Drawn Straggly and weak growth which may be caused by excessive warmth, insufficient light or growing plants too closely together.

Epiphyte A plant which grows attached to rocks or tree branches and not in soil. Many orchids and some bromeliads fall into this category.

Evergreen Plants which retain their foliage throughout the year.

Exotic This refers to plants which are not being grown in their native area but the word is often used to describe unusual or dramatically attractive plants.

Eye An undeveloped growth bud.

F1 Hybrid A plant which results from cross breeding two distinct strains.

Family A major grouping of plants which comprises genera having broadly similar characteristics.

Floret A small flower which forms part of a flower head.

Frond The leaf of a palm or fern.

Fungicide A chemical used to control fungus diseases.

Fungus A form of plant life which includes mushrooms and toadstools but also the minute organisms which cause disease in other plants.

Genus A basic botanical category which can contain from one to many hundreds of species.

Germination The start of a plant's life as the seed begins to grow.

Gesneriad A member of the Gesneriaceae family which includes many favourite houseplants . . . African violets and gloxinias etc.

Growing point The tip or leading part of a stem.

Habit The growth characteristics or general shape of a plant, e.g. trailing.

Half Hardy Describes a plant which will not survive exposure to frost.

Hardy A plant which can withstand low temperatures but not necessarily those which are extremely severe.

Herbaceous Plants which have soft and not woody growth.

Honeydew The sweet and sticky substance which is secreted by aphids and whitefly.

Hybrid A plant produced by cross breeding parents from different species, different genera and different cultivars . . . but not from different families.

Hydroponics A system of growing plants where soil is substituted by water containing dissolved nutrients.

Hygrometer An instrument for measuring the relative humidity of air.

Insecticide A chemical which kills insects.

Leggy Plant growth which is abnormally thin and tall.

Microclimate The warmth and humidity in the immediate proximity of a plant.

Neutral Medium A compost or soil which is neither acid nor alkaline.

Node The point on the stem where the leaf or sideshoot is attached.

Offset A young plant which grows from a mature specimen. It can be removed and grown separately e.g. a bulbil.

Over-potting Repotting a plant into a bigger container but one which, because it is too large, will make successful cultivation more difficult.

Peat Partially decomposed plant material, usually sedges or sphagnum moss, which is used to improve garden soil and as the basis for soil-less composts. In the United States, it is called peat moss.

Perennial A plant which can live for a number of years provided that it is grown in suitable conditions.

pH A measure of acidity and alkalinity on a scale of 1 to 14. Above 7.5 is alkaline, below 6.5 is acid and between 6.5 and 7.5 is neutral.

Pinching Out Also known as stopping, this involves removing a plant's growing tip in order to encourage the plant to break i.e. grow side-shoots.

Pip The seed of some fruits such as apples and oranges.

Pot-bound The stage when a plant's roots are completely filling the pot. In most cases repotting will be necessary.

Potting On Repotting a plant into a suitably larger container which will enable root expansion and continued development of the plant.

Pricking Out The removal of seedlings to another container so that they can be given more space to grow.

Pseudo Bulb A swollen stem which stores water and is a characteristic of many orchid species.

Rhizome An underground stem which serves the same purpose as bulbs, corms and tubers.

Root-ball The combination of roots and compost which is formed within the pot.

Runner A creeping stem which grows on the surface of the compost and will take root and form other plants.

Self-coloured Describes flowers with petals in one uniform colour.

Shrub A woody and multi-stemmed plant.

Single Flower A flower which is composed of a single layer of petals.

Spadix A flower spike which is usually surrounded by a spathe.

Spathe A bract, often coloured, which partially encloses a spadix and is exemplified in aroid plants like *Anthurium* and *Spathyphyllum*.

Species The main division in the living world which forms a sub-division of a genus.

Spore The equivalent of a seed in ferns and similar plants.

Stopping This means exactly the same as pinching out.

Strain A particular selection from a seed-raised variety.

Succulent A specialized plant which is able to withstand considerable periods of drought because of its ability to store water in fleshy leaves or stems.

Sucker A growth which arises from an underground shoot or from the plant roots.

Systemic Describes pesticides and insecticides which are absorbed by the leaves or roots of a plant. Pests and fungal growths are killed by spray contact but the systemic action continues the process from within the plant and these products can be used as preventatives.

Tender This is a description of plants which will only succeed indoors or outdoors in warm climates.

Terminal The bud, flower or shoot at the end of the stem.

Terrestrial Plants which grow in the ground.

Transpiration The natural loss of water through the leaves of a plant.

Tropical Strictly, this refers to the geographic zone which is limited by lines of latitude on either side of the equator but is commonly used to describe any plants which come from hot climates.

Tuber An underground swollen stem or root which acts as a food store and enables the plant to survive a dormant period like bulbs, corms etc.

Umbel The way the flowers are arranged on certain plants. Other forms of flower heads are spike, whorl, raceme, panicle, cyme and corymb.

Variegated Describes leaves which are patterned with contrasting colours. Usually, the background is green with white, cream, silver or gold markings.

Variety A sub-division of species.

Index